VISUAL QUICKSTART GUIDE

VBSCRIPT

FOR THE WORLD WIDE WEB

Paul Thurrott
Big Tent Media Labs

 Peachpit Press

Visual QuickStart Guide
VBScript for the World Wide Web
Paul Thurrott, Big Tent Media Labs

Peachpit Press
2414 Sixth Street
Berkeley, Ca 94710
510/548-4393
800/283-9444
510/548-5991 (fax)
http://www.peachpit.com

Peachpit Press is a division of Addison Wesley Longman

Editors: Adam Ray, Nolan Hester, Roslyn Bullas
Cover design: The Visual Group

Web site for this book: http://www.internet-nexus.com/vbvqs

ISBN 0-201-68892-1

9 8 7 6 5 4 3 2 1

Printed and bound in the United States of America

Dedication

For Joseph and Thelma White

Special thanks to Nolan Hester, Kate Reber
and the rest of the staff at Peachpit Press

Contents

CONTENTS

CONTENTS

INTRODUCTION

Congratulations! You've decided to make your Web pages more interactive, more engaging, and more interesting to those who view them. Visual Basic Script, or simply *VBScript*, is an easy way to take your Web pages to the next level. Best of all, if you understand basic HTML, you'll have no problem with VBScript. VBScript uses simple, HTML-like statements that resemble real English, not programming gobbledygook.

In this book, you will find clear, easy instructions with useful illustrations that provide everything you need to master VBScript. The beginning Web scripter can use it as a step-by-step tutorial, following along from page one to discover how scripts work with HTML. Once you are more familiar with VBScript, this book will be by your side as you work, always there when you need a reminder or quick reference.

There's a lot to learn, so let's go!

Note:

■ If you don't know *HTML*, or *Hypertext Markup Language*, you may want to learn that first. Scripting is something you can add to your knowledge after you learn HTML. For an excellent primer on HTML, check out Elizabeth Castro's *HTML for the World Wide Web: Visual QuickStart Guide*, now in its second edition from Peachpit Press.

WHY LEARN VBSCRIPT?

The World Wide Web has generated a lot of excitement, and its size, design, and technology have grown at a phenomenal rate. People spend hours online, clicking and jumping from one site to another. Thousands of people are getting online, and publishing online, every day.

And that's the problem. While the goal of any Web site is to get—and retain—users, the rapid evolution of the Web makes achieving this goal increasingly challenging. If someone jumps to one of your pages and isn't quickly entranced by what's there, it is likely that he or she will quickly leave. There are many ways to spruce up a Web page. Programs exist that let you add animation, audio, and video. Sooner or later, however, a Web designer turns to *scripting*, because of the rich functionality scripting languages offer.

This is where VBScript comes in. VBScript is scripting technology that gives your pages extra oomph so that visitors want to stay and investigate.

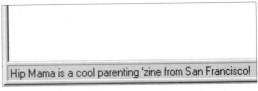

Figure i.1 Add special messages to the status bar when a visitor comes to your site.

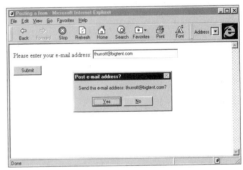

Figure i.2 With VBScript's forms and message box functions you can create a site that's useful and interactive.

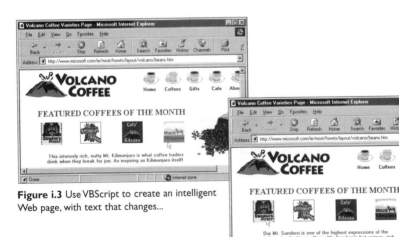

Figure i.3 Use VBScript to create an intelligent Web page, with text that changes...

...as the user's mouse passes over important parts of the screen.

WHY LEARN VBSCRIPT?

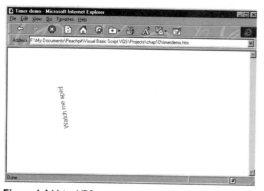

Figure i.4 Using VBScript, you can easily animate elements such as this rotating label.

WHAT DOES VBSCRIPT DO?

VBScript is a programming tool that allows you to control the layout of your pages, add effects, and get information from users in ways that aren't possible with plain HTML. VBScript takes your Web page to the next level. The end result is a Web site that's more compelling to the end user, because of its look and interactivity.

Things you can do with VBScript:

- Display messages in the status bar of the browser when a user comes, goes, or passes his or her mouse over a hyperlink.
- Automatically display the current date.
- Change formatting from visit to visit.
- Customize your Web pages with information about the user.
- Create spinning, multicolor text, and graphics.
- Create custom message boxes, dialog boxes, and alert boxes.
- Automatically display a table of contents.
- Provide real-time calculations.

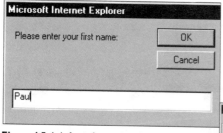

Figure i.5 Ask for information about your user....

...and reuse it later in other parts of your site.

VBSCRIPT AND JAVASCRIPT

Think of a scripting language as a watered-down programming language. You can't write your own applications with it, but you can create mini-applications that run inside a Web browser. The two most popular scripting languages, VBScript and JavaScript from Netscape, are actually subsets of programming languages. JavaScript derives from C and C++; VBScript comes from Visual Basic, the most popular programming language currently available.

One advantage of VBScript is that it is easier to read and understand simply because it is based on a programming language that was designed to be used by non-technical users. If you have ever worked with Visual Basic in any way, you will find VBScript very similar. Even if you're a first timer you will find the going easy.

VBScript can take you a long way, because it gives you access to *ActiveX*. ActiveX is a suite of Microsoft technologies that enables you to create interactive multimedia content on your site. Chapter 9 discusses ActiveX *controls*, which are pre-made pieces of code that you can simply plug into your site—for free.

Note:

■ Internet Explorer 3.0 included the first version of VBScript, as well as JScript, Microsoft's version of JavaScript. Version 2.0 shipped with Internet Explorer 4.0 and includes new built-in functions (see Chapter 2) and other high-level features. Most of these features are beyond the scope of this book.

Script i.1 You use VBScript right within the code of your HTML page. This script counts to 10 in the browser window, as shown in **Figure i.6**.

Figure i.6 VBScript in action.

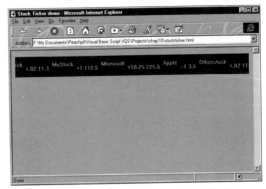

Figure i.7 VBScript gives you access to ActiveX which offers all sorts of easy-to-use gizmos, like this stock ticker.

VBSCRIPT AND JAVASCRIPT

LIMITATIONS OF VBSCRIPT

The 1996 release of Internet Explorer 3.0, and VBScript with it, was the culmination of months of work by Microsoft to turn the company into an Internet contender. Since its release, Internet Explorer has been the only real competition for Netscape's browser, Navigator. Millions of users use Internet Explorer 3.0 and 4.0.

However, as of the release of its Communicator products, and Navigator 4.0, Netscape does not support VBScript. Neither do Mac OS or UNIX-based computers. Only Windows 95 and Windows NT platforms support VBScript.

Figure i.8 The NCompass home page offer a plug-in that lets you use VBScript with Netscape browsers.

Tip

■ For users, competition is a good thing: Netscape Navigator will likely support VBScript and ActiveX in a future release. In the meantime, Netscape users can download the NCompass ScriptActive plug-in that supplies VBScript and ActiveX support now. You can find this plug-in at

http://www.ncompasslabs.com/

How to Use This Book

Throughout this book, you will learn how to design an effective Web site with VBScript. Each section has a brief introduction, which leads to a hands-on exercise. The exercises show you step-by-step how to create scripts.

The files you will make are simple HTML files, and you create them as text files in the same way you would an HTML page. Important portions of the script sections appear in red to make learning easier for you.

In this exercise, you will create a template that you should save to use while working with this book.

To create your template:

1. With a text editor of your choice, create a new, blank text file.

2. Add the HTML code as shown in **Script i.1.** Make sure to work with smart (curly) quotes off.

3. Save the file as **template.html**

Notes:

- The most exciting aspect of this book, appropriately, is on the Web itself. Check out

 http://www.internet-nexus.com/vbvqs/

 This Web site contains new features, bug fixes, additional sample code and all of the code samples you'll find in this book. Copying this code can save time and help you avoid typographical errors.

- Make sure in using a text editor that smart quotes are turned off, or your scripts won't work.

Script i.2 Make a copy of this template. You will use it in all of the exercises in this book. Important text will be highlighted in red to make your job easier.

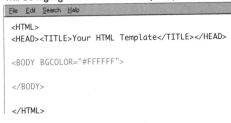

```
File  Edit  Search  Help

<HTML>
<HEAD><TITLE>Your HTML Template</TITLE></HEAD>

<BODY BGCOLOR="#FFFFFF">

</BODY>

</HTML>
```

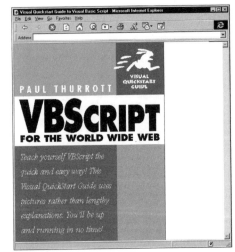

Figure i.9 Our Web site provides you with up-to-date information. This site for this book was written entirely with VBScript and ActiveX controls.

ASSUMPTIONS ABOUT YOU

Please understand that this book is written for people who already know HTML and use it to create Web sites. You don't have to be a super-HTML-coder, but you should at least understand HTML basics. This book does not use many advanced HTML features, but it does use frames, tables, and forms here and there. Absolutely no programming experience is required or expected.

Most importantly, you should want to make your Web sites better. The basic premise of this book is that building a better Web site should be easy. There are a startling number of Internet books out there that describe complex "CGI and Java Solutions," or "ActiveX Control Creation Using Visual C++" or other arcane topics or techniques no one uses anyway. Ugh. Your Web sites can be better—and will be better—with VBScript that you can learn in no time.

Enjoy!

THE BASICS

This chapter is a little different than the rest, but may be more important than most. Because there are a number of basic elements that you need to know about, this chapter contains a bit more talking and a bit less doing. Be patient. Everything here is very important. This chapter shows you what makes a script tick, and introduces basic programming terms, while giving a taste of some of the nifty built-in features of VBScript to whet your appetite.

CHOOSING AN EDITOR

The first step to working with VBScript is choosing a very important tool: the text editor you will use to write your HTML and scripts. Your choice of a text editor is highly personal, and you can use any text editor, even Microsoft Word. However, you should consider the following alternatives as well:

Windows Notepad

Notepad comes with Windows. It's free. That's where the good news stops. Notepad, often jokingly referred to as "Visual Notepad," does not allow you to load more than a single file at a time, making site management laborious. It also lacks find and replace functionality.

Programmer's File Editor

Although Programmer's File Editor (PFE) is oriented towards programming, it also makes a very good HTML editor. It can handle any number of simultaneously open files and includes all the cut and paste, find and replace, and automatic indenting you'll ever want. Best yet, it's free.

SitePad

SitePad is designed for HTML and VRML editing, and it offers syntax coloring and syntax checking for HTML, VBScript, and JavaScript. The full version costs $40, but it's well worth it if you're serious about HTML editing and Web scripting.

ActiveX Control Pad

Microsoft's ActiveX Control Pad offers rudimentary text editing features, but excels at adding ActiveX controls and scripting to your Web pages. This tool is covered in Chapter 10.

Other Editors

For a more complete list of HTML editors with URLs for all those mentioned here, please refer this book's Web site:

http://www.internet-nexus.com/vbvqs

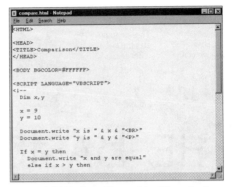

Figure 1.1 Windows Notepad in all its splendor.

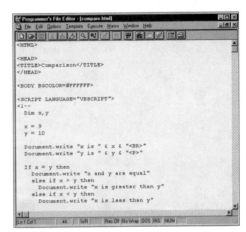

Figure 1.2 PFE is a full-featured text editor that is worth considering. Download it from **http://www.lancs.ac.uk/people/cpaap/pfe/**

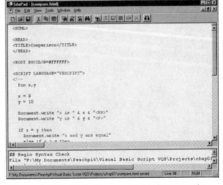

Figure 1.3 SitePad offers syntax coloring and is designed specifically for HTML editing. Download it from **http://www.sni.net/express**

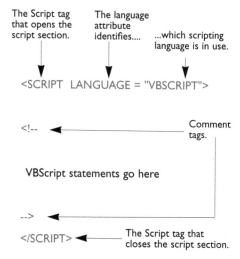

The Script tag that opens the script section.

The language attribute identifies....

...which scripting language is in use.

```
<SCRIPT LANGUAGE = "VBSCRIPT">
```

```
<!--
```
Comment tags.

VBScript statements go here

```
-->
```

```
</SCRIPT>
```
The Script tag that closes the script section.

Figure 1.4 A script section and its parts.

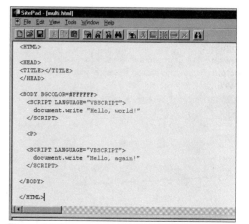

Figure 1.5 You can put multiple script sections in a single document.

INTRODUCING THE SCRIPT SECTION

You only need to know a few new HTML tags to get going with scripting. For the most part, all of the VBScript you create will be contained within the **<SCRIPT>** and **</SCRIPT>** tags, in what is called a *script section*. **Figure 1.4** shows the basic parts of a script section.

Quick facts about script sections:

- Notice that the code does not use smart (curly) quotes. Never use smart quotes in your code or you'll get an error message.

- An HTML document can contain more than one script section.

- VBScript statements usually execute in order, as the browser encounters them. This type of scripting is called *direct execution*. In Chapter 2, you will learn about *deferred scripting* using subroutines, which means that the scripts execute by reference, without regard to their order in the code.

- Script sections can either appear in the *body section*, that is between the **<BODY>** and **</BODY>** tags, or above the body section.

- The **LANGUAGE** attribute in this book will always read **VBSCRIPT** but JavaScript code can also be entered in a script section. If this is the case, the **LANGUAGE** attribute will read **JAVASCRIPT**.

- The **<!--** and **-->** comment tags prevent browsers that are incompatible with Visual Basic scripting from attempting to execute the code between the **<SCRIPT>** tags. If you leave them out, users with incompatible browsers will encounter errors.

INTRODUCING THE SCRIPT SECTION

OBJECTS, PROPERTIES, AND METHODS

In the most basic sense, VBScript relies on objects, properties, and methods to work its magic. *Objects* are the elements of the programming language that identify the things you see on a Web page, such as a browser window, a button, or a hyperlink. Each object has properties. *Properties* are attributes, such as height or width. Finally, every object has *methods*, or things it can do, such as open or close.

Figure 1.6 shows an example of a basic script that uses VBScript objects, properties, and methods. In writing code, you combine objects with methods and properties by using a period. This format is called dot notation, as shown in **Figure 1.7.** Later chapters cover objects and what they can do in more detail.

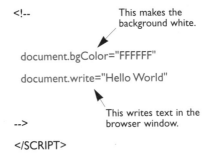

```
<SCRIPT  LANGUAGE = "VBSCRIPT">

<!--                          This makes the
                              background white.

    document.bgColor="FFFFFF"

    document.write="Hello World"

                              This writes text in the
-->                           browser window.

</SCRIPT>
```

Figure 1.6 An object with its method and properties. In this case, the object is the document you are working on. Its background property is white, and its method is writing text.

Figure 1.7 Dot notation is used to access an object's properties, in this case the **name** property of the **Window** object.

Figure 1.8 This is the blank HTML file that will serve as the container for your first script.

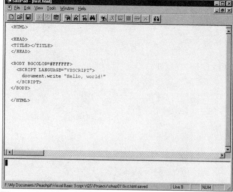

Figure 1.9 Your HMTL file should look like this when the script code is entered.

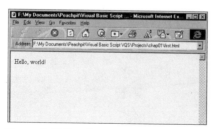

Figure 1.10 Your first script running in Internet Explorer.

WRITING YOUR FIRST SCRIPT

It's time, at last, to write your first VBscript. As you might expect, you must first create an HTML file that will contain the script. If you don't see the proper results when you load the final file in the browser, or if you receive a script error dialog box, check that you entered the script exactly as shown.

To write your first script:

1. Using your HTML editor, enter the following code:

   ```
   <HTML>

   <HEAD>

   <TITLE></TITLE>

   </HEAD>

   <BODY BGCOLOR=#FFFFFF>

   </BODY>

   </HTML>
   ```

2. Save the file as first.html

3. Directly after the <BODY> tag, enter the following script section:

   ```
   <SCRIPT LANGUAGE="VBSCRIPT">

      document.write "Hello, world!"

   </SCRIPT>
   ```

4. Save the file and load it in your browser.

Note:

■ Make sure you are not working with smart quotes or the browser will return an error message.

LIVING WITH ERRORS

In scripting, as in life, we all make errors, and if you have worked with HTML much, you know how painstaking the process of writing code and debugging can be. Fortunately, your browser has an *error message dialog box* that tries to identify what you have done wrong. Sometimes this message can be pretty useful.

To see the error message dialog box:

1. Change the second line of the script so that it reads:

   document.write Hello, world!"

2. Save the file as **error.html** and reload it in Internet Explorer. The dialog box shown in **Figure 1.11** appears.

3. Click the OK button to remove the dialog and the page will load, minus the script.

Tip:

- When your scripts get longer you can use these messages to pinpoint errors. The rule of thumb here is to read the message and act on it if you can. If not, locate the line it complains about and try to find the error yourself.

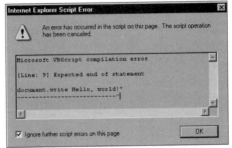

Figure 1.11 In this case, it's hard to tell what Internet Explorer is trying to tell you. You left the first quote off the **Hello, world!** string, but the dialog is pointing to the end of the line and mentions that it expected to find an **End of Statement**. At least it's pointing to the line that contains the error, and that will give you a place to start.

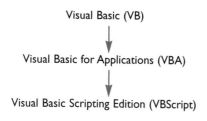

Visual Basic (VB)

↓

Visual Basic for Applications (VBA)

↓

Visual Basic Scripting Edition (VBScript)

Figure 1.12 VBScript is a subset of VBA and VB.

CREATING VARIABLES

Since VBScript is based on Visual Basic, it inherited many of its parent's conventions. All programming languages have ways of dealing with data, defining variables and constants, dealing with mathematical operators, and commenting within source code to make it more readable. *Variables* are containers for data. For example:

```
For x = 0 to 10
    Document.write x & "<BR>"
Next
```

This code makes use of a variable, called **x**. In this case, the variable **x** is used to simply hold values for a counter. In fact, you could have called the variable **counter**:

```
For counter = 0 to 10
    Document.write counter & "<BR>"
Next
```

Tips on naming variables:

- Variable names must start with a letter, cannot contain a period and cannot exceed 255 characters.
- You cannot use two variables with the same name in the same code section; the names must be unique.
- You cannot use words such as **For** and **Next** that have a specific use within the VBScript language.
- Avoid single-letter variable names unless they appear in a loop, like **x** in the example above.
- Create descriptive names. You can use mixed case (though VBScript ignores case) to make the name more readable as well. Names like **Visitor**, **NewValue**, and **Count** are good examples.

DECLARING VARIABLES

To use a variable, you must first *declare* it. This just means that you give it a name and let VBScript know you'll be using it. You declare a variable using a keyword. A *keyword* is a word, like **For** or **Next**, that has a specific use in the VBScript language. In this case, the keyword to declare a variable is **Dim**. An example looks like:

    Dim x

    For x = 0 to 10

        Document.Write x & "<BR>"

    Next

Imagine that you want to create a script that receives a temperature in Fahrenheit from the user and converts it to Celsius. **Figure 1.13** shows an example of this script.

A variable exists solely to hold a value. This may be something you receive from the user, or something that you name in your code with an equal (=) sign:

    Dim Count

    Dim Name

    Count = 0

    Name = "Stephanie"

Tip:

- You can declare multiple variables with the same **Dim** statement, instead of using multiple **Dim** statements, one for each variable. For example, the code

    Dim Count

    Dim Name

    Dim Phone

    can be shortened like this by separating each variable name with a comma:

    Dim Count, Name, Phone

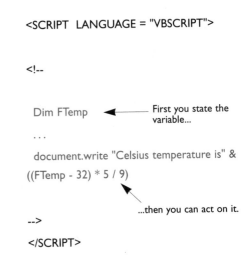

```
<SCRIPT  LANGUAGE = "VBSCRIPT">


<!--


    Dim FTemp        ◄──── First you state the
                          variable...
    . . .

    document.write "Celsius temperature is" &
    ((FTemp - 32) * 5 / 9)
                          ↖
                              ...then you can act on it.
-->

</SCRIPT>
```

Figure 1.13 This script takes a value, converts it to Celsius and prints it to the screen. Note that this isn't a complete example, because you need first to receive the variable from the user. Chapter 2 shows you how to use form boxes to build that sort of interactivity into your pages.

DECLARING VARIABLES

```
<SCRIPT LANGUAGE = "VBSCRIPT">

<!--

Const INCHES, PI

INCHES = 12

PI = 3.14

For x = 0 to INCHES

. . .

Next

-->

</SCRIPT>
```

Figure 1.14 This code section establishes the constant values for inches and for Pi.

USING CONSTANTS

Constants are similar to variables in that they are named values. The difference, however, is that *constants* establish an initial value that never changes. You use a constant any time you are working with a value that doesn't change, like Pi, or the number of inches in a foot.

The keyword **const** is used to declare constants. To help you distinguish constants from variables, name your constants with all capital letters.

You will encounter variables and constants throughout this book, and their use will be more apparent as you gain experience with them.

USING OPERATORS

VBScript allows the use of numerous operators. *Operators* are symbols that specify certain actions, such as addition or subtraction. **Table 1.1** lists the operators and what they do.

You use operators in expressions. *Expressions* are simply a combination of operators and other values. These values can be variables, constants, or even functions. Consider this line of code:

    Document.write Count + 1

This code adds 1 to **Count** and outputs the result. The code **Count + 1** is an operation involving two values that uses the *addition* operator.

Table 1.1 The VB Script Operators.

OPERATOR	WHAT IT DOES
+	addition
-	subtraction or unary negation
*	multiplication
/	division
\	integer division: returns the integer part of a division
MOD	modulo: returns the remainder of a division.
^	exponentiation: raises a number to a power
&	string concatenation
=	equal
< >	not equal
<	less than
>	greater than
<=	less than or equal to
>=	greater than or equal to
is	equivalent object

Tips

- Operators are generally used for arithmetic, comparison, and other operations. At least some of the arithmetic operators are probably pretty obvious.

- The **&** operator *concatenates*, or joins, two strings. **Script 1.1** provides an example.

- The *comparison* operators allow you to compare two values. It returns a **True** or **False** value, based on the result of the comparison. Using the comparison operators is like asking a question. For example, the following comparison asks whether **x** and **y** are equal.

    If x = y then

        Document.write "x and y are equal"

    If they are equal, the string **x and y are equal** will be printed out.

Script 1.1 The value of **x** is concatenated with the **
** tag. The result is that the value of **x** is printed out followed by a line break. This sort of concatenation is useful when using the **document.write** function you will see throughout this book.

```
File  Edit  Search  Help

<HTML>
<HEAD><TITLE>Title of page</TITLE></HEAD>
  Dim x
  For x = 0 to 10
    Document.Write x & "<BR>"
  Next


<BODY>

</HTML>
```

```
<SCRIPT  LANGUAGE = "VBSCRIPT">

<!--


' Use X as a counter variable

' Name identifies the user

Rem this is a comment too!


Dim X, Name



-->

</SCRIPT>
```

Figure 1.15 This code section shows the two types of comments, one initiated by the apostrophe ('), the other by the keyword **Rem.**

ADDING COMMENTS

The VBScript comment is a final bit of background that you should understand. Historically, comments have been used by programmers to let others reading the code understand what they were up to. Comments also helpful for the programmer when he or she returns to the code months—or years—later and can't remember what it does.

Commenting your code is very important, especially if you are doing something fairly complex. VBScript allows you to use the keyword **Rem** (for "remark") or the apostrophe (') to denote comments.

Everything after **Rem** or ' that appears on the same line is considered a comment and will be ignored by the browser.

Tip:

■ Remember, save time and prevent aggravation by using comments in your scripts. You'll be happy you did.

Working with Subroutines

2

Up to this point, your scripts have been used just like HTML tags—they run, or *execute*, in sequence as the page loads from top to bottom. You can also introduce blocks of code once and then refer to them from within your HTML page. This type of code is called a *subroutine*. Subroutines offer a number of benefits. Since you only state a piece of code once, there may be less typing. Subroutines also make your code easier to maintain and change, since you only need to change the one piece of code, not all the times that the code actually executes.

This chapter introduces you to the two kinds of subroutines: procedures and functions. You will learn how subroutines work and how they pass parameters. The second part of the chapter shows you some of the more interesting built-in functions and how to put them to work.

DEFINING AND CALLING PROCEDURES

You can place the code for a procedure anywhere in a script because it executes only when called. For the sake of consistency, you should probably place all script sections before, or above, the body section of an HTML page.

To define a procedure:

1. Create a blank HTML file and save it as firstproc.html

2. Add the script section before the <BODY> tag, as shown in **Script 2.1**.

In order for the procedure to appear on the Web page, you should reference it with a statement in the body of the code, or *call* the procedure.

To call a procedure:

1. Add the code that uses the **Call** keyword along with the name of the procedure with the body section of the HTML file, as shown in **Script 2.2**.

2. Save the file and load the page in your browser. The result should resemble **Figure 2.1**.

Tip:

- The **Call** keyword is optional. This code would work with just the name of the parameter being named in the body.

- You may be saying, "Hey, I could do this in HTML!" True. But remember, this is your first procedure.

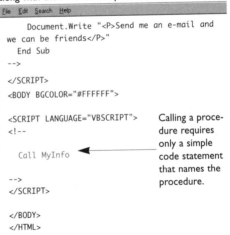

Figure 2.1 Sure, you could do this in HTML, but just wait until we make things a bit more complicated.

Script 2.1 A procedure must start with the keyword **Sub,** followed by the name of the procedure, **MyInfo()** and what that procedure will do. In this case, **MyInfo()** writes three lines of text.

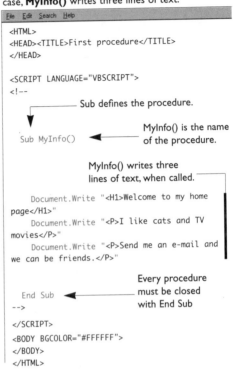

Script 2.2 To call a procedure, use the **Call** keyword along with the name of the procedure.

```
File  Edit  Search  Help
      Document.Write "<P>Send me an e-mail and
we can be friends</P>"
   End Sub
-->

</SCRIPT>
<BODY BGCOLOR="#FFFFFF">

<SCRIPT LANGUAGE="VBSCRIPT">
<!--

      Call MyInfo

-->
</SCRIPT>

</BODY>
</HTML>
```

Calling a procedure requires only a simple code statement that names the procedure.

Script 2.3 Parameters appear in the parentheses after the procedure.

```
File  Edit  Search  Help

<HTML>
<HEAD><TITLE>Parameters</TITLE></HEAD>
<SCRIPT LANGUAGE="VBSCRIPT">
<!--                         MyInfo() contains
                             three parameters...

   Sub MyInfo(First, Second, Third)
      Document.Write First & Second & Third
   End Sub
-->                          which it prints to
</SCRIPT>                     the browser window
<BODY BGCOLOR="#FFFFFF">
</BODY>
</HTML>
```

Script 2.4 Parameter passing allows you to work on multiple sets of variables with specific variable names. In order to call the function, you must create a list of variables to pass to the procedures, using a **Dim** statement.

```
File  Edit  Search  Help

<HTML>
<HEAD><TITLE>Parameters</TITLE></HEAD>
<SCRIPT LANGUAGE="VBSCRIPT">
<!--
   Sub MyInfo(First, Second, Third)
      Document.Write First & Second & Third
   End Sub
-->
</SCRIPT>

<BODY BGCOLOR="#FFFFFF">
<SCRIPT LANGUAGE="VBSCRIPT">
<!--
   Dim Title, Line1, Line2

   Title = "<H1>Welcome to my home page.</H1>"
   Line1 = "<P>I like cats and TV movies.</P>"
   Line2 = "<P>Send me an e-mail and we can be
friends.</P>"

   Call MyInfo (Title, Line1, Line2)

   Dim Title, Line1, Line2

   Title2 = "<H1>Before you leave</H1>"
   Line3 = "<P>Don't forget to sign my
guestbook.</P>"
   Line4 = "<P>Tell me some movies you like.</P>"

   Call MyInfo (Title2, Line3, Line4)

-->
</SCRIPT>
</BODY>
</HTML>
```

USING PARAMETERS

Procedures allow you to include multiple variables, called *parameters*, or arguments. Remember, the benefit of creating procedures is being able to reuse code. Parameters are generic. *Parameter passing* is the process of passing specific variables to generic parameters within your procedure.

To define a subroutine with parameters:

1. Create a blank HTML file. Save this file as params.html

2. Add the script section above the <BODY> tag, as shown in **Script 2.3.**

Now you call the procedure. To do this, follow the procedure name with a list of variables that match the parameter list in the function body.

To call a subroutine with parameters:

1. Add a script section within the body section, as shown in **Script 2.4,** and save the file.

2. Load the page into your browser. The result should resemble **Figure 2.2.**

Figure 2.2 Passing parameters allows you to reuse code, a practice that can save a lot of time.

USING FUNCTIONS

Functions are subroutines—or callable blocks of code—just like procedures. They also may have parameters (also known as arguments) that receive values when the function is called. **Script 2.5** shows the parts of a function.

Functions differ in that they can return a single value. This difference means that functions can be used in expressions, such as addition or subtraction. This is simpler than it may sound. Let's look at some examples. Here is a function that calculates the square of a number that is passed to it as a parameter.

```
Function MySquare (Num)

  MySquare = Num * Num

End Function
```

Because functions return a single value, you can use **MySquare** in an expression like

```
x = x + MySquare(x)
```

In this case, the variable **x** equals its previous value plus its square. Basically, you can use the function's return value just as you would use any variable:

```
Document.Write MySquare(6)
```

This will output 36.

You call functions in the same way that you call procedures: with an optional **Call** statement followed by the name of the function and any parameter values to be passed.

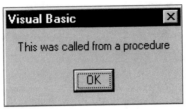

Figure 2.3 VBScript comes with many built-in functions that handle common tasks associated with numbers, time, dates, strings and more. This **MsgBox** is a good example of a built-in function. The use of your own functions and of the built-in functions is covered in the following pages.

Script 2.5 A function uses the keyword **Function**. Like procedures, functions work with parameters, and conclude with an **End** statement.

```
File  Edit  Search  Help

<HTML>
<HEAD><TITLE>Title of page</TITLE></HEAD>
<SCRIPT LANGUAGE="VBSCRIPT">
<!--

Function <function_name> (parameter1, parameter2)
   VBScript code goes here
End Function

-->
</SCRIPT>
<BODY BGCOLOR="FFFFFF">
```

Script 2.6 This function contains two parameters, which it joins—or concatenates—together.

```
File  Edit  Search  Help

<HTML>
<HEAD><TITLE>Functions</TITLE></HEAD>
<SCRIPT LANGUAGE="VBSCRIPT">
<!--
    Function Concat (String1, String2)
      Concat = String1 & String2
    End Function
-->
</SCRIPT>
<BODY BGCOLOR="#FFFFFF">
</BODY>
</HTML>
```

Script 2.7 The actual **Call** keyword is optional. Just naming the function **Concat** is enough to pass the parameters.

```
File  Edit  Search  Help

<HTML>
<HEAD><TITLE>Functions</TITLE></HEAD>
<SCRIPT LANGUAGE="VBSCRIPT">
<!--
    Function Concat (String1, String2)
      Concat = String1 & String2
    End Function
-->
</SCRIPT>
<BODY BGCOLOR="#FFFFFF">
<SCRIPT LANGUAGE="VBSCRIPT">
<!--
    Document.Write Concat ("Bird", "Brain") &
"<BR>"
    Document.Write Concat ("VB", "Script") & "<BR>"
-->
</SCRIPT>
</BODY>
</HTML>
```

To define a function:

1. Create a blank HTML file and save it as firstfunc.html

2. In a script section before the body section, add a function, as shown in **Script 2.6,** which joins—or *concatenates*—two strings.

To call a function:

1. Create a script section within the body section of the HTML file, as shown in

   Script 2.7.

2. Save the file and load it in your browser. As shown in **Figure 2.4,** the Concat function joins each set of variables.

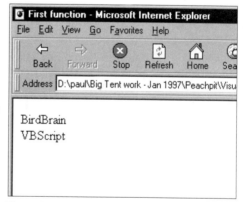

Figure 2.4 The **Concat** function is called twice in this example. It joins together two sets of text strings.

USING FUNCTIONS

Using Form Buttons

VBScript includes handy buttons that you can create, label, and control. Not only do these buttons save you time, they also give your pages a uniform and professional look and feel. There are three basic form buttons: a submit button, a reset button, and a plain button that you can customize. Once you know how to create form buttons, you can add functionality to them with VBScript.

To create form buttons:

1. Create a new HTML file and save it as buttons.html

2. Add code to the body section as shown in **Script 2.8.**

3. Save the file and load it into your browser. The result should look like **Figure 2.5.**

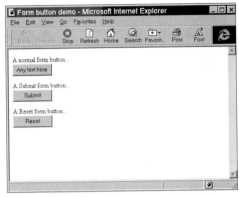

Figure 2.5 VBScript comes with three form buttons.

Script 2.8 VBScript gives you a powerful and easy way to create, label, and control command buttons.

```
File   Edit   Search   Help

<HTML>
<HEAD><TITLE>Form buttons</TITLE></HEAD>

<BODY BGCOLOR="#FFFFFF">

<FORM>
   A normal form button...
   <BR><INPUT TYPE="BUTTON" VALUE="Any text here">

   <BR><BR>
   A Submit form button...
   <BR><INPUT TYPE="Submit">

   <BR><BR>
   A Reset form button...
   <BR><INPUT TYPE="Reset">

</FORM>

</BODY>
</HTML>
```

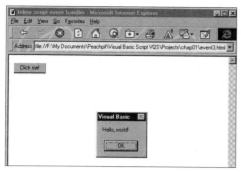

Figure 2.6 Built-in functions such as this message box are easy to use and can save you a lot of time.

Script 2.9 Form buttons are only really useful when you attach a script to them.

```
File  Edit  Search  Help
<HTML>
<HEAD><TITLE>Message boxes</TITLE></HEAD>

<BODY BGCOLOR="#FFFFFF">

<FORM>
    <INPUT TYPE=Button NAME=Button1 VALUE="Click
Me!">
</FORM>

</BODY>
</HTML>
```

Script 2.10 Place the script section for the message box right above the form button code.

```
File  Edit  Search  Help
<HTML>
<HEAD><TITLE>Message boxes</TITLE></HEAD>

<BODY BGCOLOR="#FFFFFF">

<SCRIPT LANGUAGE="VBSCRIPT" EVENT="OnClick"
FOR="Button1">
<!--
    MsgBox "Hello, world!"
-->
</SCRIPT>

<FORM>
    <INPUT TYPE=Button NAME=Button1 VALUE="Click
Me!"
</FORM>

</BODY>
</HTML>
```

BUILT-IN FUNCTIONS

Earlier in the chapter, you learned how to use functions. While they may be interesting conceptually, creating functions can be time consuming. Fortunately, VBScript comes with dozens of useful built-in functions that you can use immediately. These functions handle all sorts of things, from date and time conversions to number crunching. **MsgBox**, and the related **InputBox**, both provide pop-up dialog boxes and work together with the built-in form buttons quite handily.

To create a form button:

1. Create a new HTML file and save it as msgbox.html

2. Add the code in the body section, as shown in **Script 2.9,** to create a form button.

3. Add code for the built-in message box function above the form button script, as shown in **Script 2.10.**

4. Save the file and view it in your browser. The result should look like **Figure 2.6.**

Tips:

- VBScript Version 2.0, which shipped with Internet Explorer 4.0, introduced a number of new built-in functions. A complete list of VBScript functions can be found on this book's Web site at:

    http://www.internet-nexus.com/vbvqs/

- The following sections cover a few of the more interesting built-in functions.

BUILT-IN FUNCTIONS

19

DATE AND TIME FUNCTIONS

You have probably seen Web sites that display the current date and time and wondered how they did it. VBScript comes with numerous built-in date and time functions. The key to working with these functions is knowing how to use them together to get the date and time in a form that you like. **Table 2.1** shows some of the built-in time and date functions. Check the VBScript built-in function reference on this book's Web site for details.

To add the date to a page:

1. Create a blank HTML file and save it as getdate.html

2. Create a script section before the body section that defines a function called **GetDate**, as shown in **Script 2.11.**

3. Within the body section call **GetDate**, as shown in **Script 2.12.**

4. Save the file and load it in your browser. The result should resemble **Figure 2.7.**

Note:

- VBScript 2.0 introduced the MonthName built-in function feature with Explorer 4.0. Chapter 7 explains how to format the date for older browsers.

Table 2.1 These are just a select group of the date and time functions. To see a more comprehensive list check out **http://www.internet-nexus.com/vbvqs**

FUNCTION	EXAMPLE
Now	10/29/1997 01:33:48 AM
Date	10/29/1997
Time	01:33:48 AM
Year	1997
Month	10
MonthName	October
Day	29

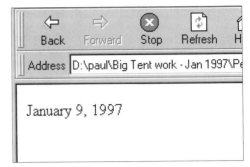

Figure 2.7 The date functions allow you to create a professional-looking date display.

Script 2.11 You can handle the format of the date by stringing together the different date functions. Notice the **False** following **MonthName.** If you change this to **True,** the month will appear as a three letter abbreviation.

```
File  Edit  Search  Help
<HTML>
<HEAD><TITLE>Getting the Date</TITLE></HEAD>

<SCRIPT LANGUAGE = "VBSCRIPT">
<!--
    Function GetDate()
        Dim MyMonthName

        MyMonthName = MonthName(Month(Now), False)
        GetDate = MyMonthName & " " & Day(Now) & ", "
& Year(Now)
        End Function1
-->
</SCRIPT>
<BODY BGCOLOR="#FFFFFF">
</BODY>
</HTML>
```

Script 2.12 Calling the date requires a simple script.

```
File  Edit  Search  Help
        MyMonthName = MonthName(Month(Now), False)
        GetDate = MyMonthName & " " & Day(Now) & ", "
& Year(Now)
        End Function1
-->
</SCRIPT>
<BODY BGCOLOR="#FFFFFF">
<SCRIPT LANGUAGE = "VBSCRIPT">
<!--
    Document.Write GetDate
-->
</SCRIPT>
</BODY>
</HTML>
```

Script 2.13 Randomize initializes VBScript's built-in random number generator. **Rnd** returns a value between 0 and 1. **Int** is another built-in function that returns any parameter it receives as an integer. **Greeting (5)** creates a preset list that contains five options.

```
File  Edit  Search  Help

<HTML>
<HEAD><TITLE>Random messages</TITLE></HEAD>
<SCRIPT LANGUAGE = "VBSCRIPT">
<!--

  Function RandomGreeting()
    Dim Greeting(5), Quote

    Randomize

    Greeting(0) = "Hello there!"
    Greeting(1) = "Welcome!"
    Greeting(2) = "Bienvenido!"
    Greeting(3) = "Hola!"
    Greeting(4) = "Enjoy your stay!"

    Quote = Int(Rnd() * ((5 - 1) + 1))
    RandomGreeting = Greeting(Quote)
  End Function
-->
</SCRIPT>
<BODY BGCOLOR="#FFFFFF">
</BODY>
</HTML>
```

CREATING RANDOM MESSAGES

VBScript contains a number of built-in math functions that a Web designer can put to good use. The **Rnd** function is a fine example. The **Rnd** function automatically returns a value between 0 and 1. You can use this function along with the **Int** function to randomly choose and display messages to your user from a preset list, also called an *array*.

To use the built-in math functions:

1. Create a blank HTML file and save it as random.html

2. Add a script section before the body section, as shown in **Script 2.13**.

3. Now, add a script section inside the body section, as shown in **Script 2.14**.

4. Save the file and load it in your browser. Every time you reload the page, the quote will change randomly. The result should resemble **Figure 2.8**.

Script 2.14 Add this simple script within the body section.

```
File  Edit  Search  Help

    Greeting(3) = "Hola!"
    Greeting(4) = "Enjoy your stay!"

    Quote = Int(Rnd() * ((5 - 1) + 1))
    RandomGreeting = Greeting(Quote)
  End Function
-->
</SCRIPT>
<BODY BGCOLOR="#FFFFFF">
<SCRIPT LANGUAGE = "VBSCRIPT">
<!--
  Document.Write RandomGreeting
-->
</SCRIPT>
</BODY>
</HTML>
```

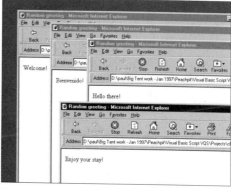

Figure 2.8 Random welcome quotes using the Randomize statement and the **Rnd** and **Int** functions.

CONTROLLING TEXT FORMATS

The *string functions* allow you to control the format of text and display it in different ways in the browser window. Using VBScript to control text formatting reduces the chance of typographical errors. The **Ucase** function, for example, converts a string to all uppercase letters, while the **Lcase** function converts a string to all lowercase letters. **Table 2.2** shows some of the string functions. String functions also allow you to separate and represent text, which can eliminate hand coding text as well.

To use the built-in string functions:

1. Create a blank HTML file and save it as strings.html

2. Add a script section to the file, above the body section, as shown in **Script 2.15.**

3. Now, add the script within the body section, as shown in **Script 2.16** and save the file.

4. Load the page in your browser. Your result should resemble **Figure 2.9.**

Script 2.16 This script defines the three strings of text from which **Chew** pulls characters.

```
File  Edit  Search  Help

<BODY #FFFFFF>
<SCRIPT LANGUAGE="VBSCRIPT">
<!--
   Document.Write "<B>You're so ugly</B>"
   Call Chew("You're so ugly")

   Document.Write "<P><B>I could press your face
in dough</B>"
   Call Chew("I could press your face in dough")

   Document.Write "<P><B>and make gorilla
cookies!</B>"
   Call Chew("and make gorilla cookies!")
-->
</SCRIPT>
</BODY>
</HTML>
```

Table 2.2 The string functions allow you to control the presentation of text.

FUNCTION	WHAT IT DOES
Ucase	converts all text to uppercase
Lcase	converts all text to lowercase
Left	extracts part of a string from the left side
Right	extracts part of a string from the right side
Mid	extracts part of a string from the middle

Script 2.15 Create a function called **Chew** which will separate a portion of characters from the left, right, and middle. The **Mid** function works with the length parameter, **Len**, to determine the number of characters to extract.

```
File  Edit  Search  Help

<HTML>
<HEAD><TITLE>String Functions</TITLE></HEAD>
<SCRIPT LANGUAGE="VBSCRIPT">
<!--
   Sub Chew(theString)
      Document.Write "<BR>The leftmost 3
characters are <I>" & Left(theString, 3) &
"</I>"

      Document.Write "<BR>The rightmost 3
characters are <I>" & Right(theString, 3) &
"</I>"

      Document.Write "<BR>The middle 3
characters are <I>" & Mid(theString,
(Len(theString)/2) - 3, 3) & "</I>"

   End Sub
-->
</SCRIPT>
<BODY BGCOLOR="#FFFFFF">
</BODY>
</HTML>
```

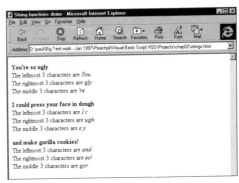

Figure 2.9 An homage to Redd Foxx, thanks to VBScript's built-in string functions.

MsgBox(prompt[, buttons][, title]

[, helpfile, context])

Figure 2.10 Both **MsgBox** and **InputBox** can work with a number of parameters: prompt, buttons, title, helpfile, and context. The square brackets around some of the parameters mean they are optional. **Table 2.3** shows what each of these parameters can do.

Table 2.3 The parameters that work with **MsgBox** and **Input Box.**

PARAMETER	WHAT IT DOES
buttons	determines the buttons that appear in the dialog box. See Table 2.3 for a list of the buttons you can call
title	displays the title of the dialog box; presents the type of browser by default
helpfile	displays the name of the file that provides online help
context	displays the context from which the user is coming to the helpfile

Table 2.4 The buttons and return values of **MsgBox** and **Input Box.**

BUTTON	RETURN VALUE
vbOK	The OK button was pressed.
vbCancel	The Cancel button was pressed.
vbAbort	The Abort button was pressed.
vbRetry	The Retry button was pressed.
vbIgnore	The Ignore button was pressed.
vbYes	The Yes button was pressed.
vbNo	The No button was pressed.

MORE ON MESSAGE AND INPUT BOXES

Of VBScript's built-in functions, the message and input box functions may be the most frequently used. MsgBox displays a message in a pop-up window called a *dialog box* that offers the user a variety of options. InputBox is very similar, except that it allows you to accept a string of text from the user. Both of these functions accept a number of parameters, shown in **Figure 2.10.**

MsgBox also has some unique return values that identify which button the user pressed to close the dialog box. The return value, then, can help you make decisions based on the button that was pressed. **Table 2.4** identifies the possible return values and the button that was pressed for each return value.

You will learn about decision-making code in the next chapter and use it along with a message box to respond to user requests.

Using Loops
and Conditions

3

VBScript statements normally execute in the sequence they appear in your code. The time will come, however, when you will want to change the order that VBScript executes lines of code. Fortunately, VBScript allows you to do just this, using conditional code execution and looping constructs. These are big words that describe simple concepts, so don't be put off by the terms. *Conditional code execution* is simply the process of making a decision, and *looping constructs* allow you to execute blocks of code over and over again. This chapter is concerned with these two concepts and the ways that you can change the flow of code execution with them.

MAKING DECISIONS

One of the primary benefits of VBScript is that you can use it to help you make decisions. These decisions can be based on questions you ask the user, or even based on information about the browser he or she is using to view your site. VBScript, like other programming languages, supports a way to execute certain blocks of code based on a decision.

Programming language purists call this sort of activity *conditional code execution*. The aim here is simply to write code that executes when you want it to. VBScript has several ways to accomplish this, using features of the VBScript language. **Table 3.1** shows the code statements that allow you to make decisions.

The simplest conditional statement involves two keywords, **If** and **Then. Figure 3.1** shows how these keywords work. If there are lines of code after the one beginning with **If**, you need to use the **End If** statement, as shown in **Figure 3.2.** You also use **End If** when you want to execute more than a single line of code.

Table 3.1 These pieces of code allow you to make decisions with increasing levels of complexity.

CONDITION	WHAT IT DOES
If-Then	makes a simple decision
If-Then-Else	makes a decision with an alternative
If-Then-ElseIf	makes a decision with multiple alternatives
Select Case	makes a decision with a long list of possible outcomes

```
If condition Then VBScript statements
```

Figure 3.1 If-Then statements create the simplest type of decision, involving only one condition. **If** the condition part is true, **Then** the VBScript statements that follow are executed.

```
If Age > 21 Then

    Document.Write "You are old enough
to know better."

    Document.Write "<BR>You are old
enough to drink."

End If
```

Figure 3.2 When lines of code follow an **If-Then** statement, you need to include an **End If** statement.

MAKING DECISIONS

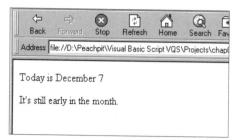

Figure 3.3 Your script checks the current date and makes a decision about which code to execute.

Script 3.1 This example makes a simple decision about the date and about whether to declare something on the page.

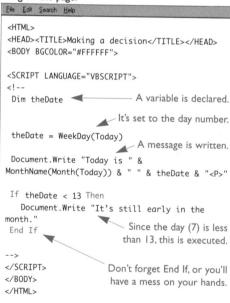

```
File  Edit  Search  Help

<HTML>
<HEAD><TITLE>Making a decision</TITLE></HEAD>
<BODY BGCOLOR="#FFFFFF">

<SCRIPT LANGUAGE="VBSCRIPT">
<!--
  Dim theDate        ◀——— A variable is declared.
                          ◀— It's set to the day number.
  theDate = WeekDay(Today)
                          ◀— A message is written.
  Document.Write "Today is " &
MonthName(Month(Today)) & " " & theDate & "<P>"

  If theDate < 13 Then
     Document.Write "It's still early in the
month."
  End If               ◀— Since the day (7) is less
                          than 13, this is executed.
-->
</SCRIPT>               Don't forget End If, or you'll
</BODY>                 have a mess on your hands.
</HTML>
```

To create a simple decision:

1. Create a blank HTML file. Save the file as decision.html

2. Add a script section in the body section, as shown in **Script 3.1.**

3. Save the file and load it in your browser. The result should resemble **Figure 3.3.**

Tips:

- Using the **And** keyword, you can perform more complex decision making on a single line. **And** is an operator that allows you to perform a logical decision, as shown in **Script 3.2.** The method has the drawback of causing your script to execute unnecessary code.

- For more information on working with the built-in date and time functions, check out Chapter 2.

Script 3.2 The statement after the line of code that contains the **And** executes only if the code statements before and after it are true.

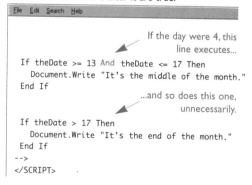

```
File  Edit  Search  Help
                          If the day were 4, this
                             line executes...
  If theDate >= 13 And theDate <= 17 Then
     Document.Write "It's the middle of the month."
  End If
                          ...and so does this one,
                             unnecessarily.
  If theDate > 17 Then
     Document.Write "It's the end of the month."
  End If
-->
</SCRIPT>
```

MORE COMPLEX DECISIONS

If-Then statements allow you to make simple decisions, and stringing multiple statements together is one way to build more complex decision making into your code. The problem with this approach is that each If-Then block executes, regardless of whether a previous section was determined to be true, thus burdening your script and making it run more slowly.

If you're thinking that there must be a better way, you're right. VBScript also supports the Else clause in an If-Then, making the whole statement an If-Then-Else clause, as shown in **Figure 3.4.** VBScript also supports ElseIf, as shown in **Figure 3.5,** which allows you to combine numerous groups of statements.

To create more complex decisions:

1. Create an HTML file. Save the file as decision2.html

2. Add a script section in the body, as shown in **Script 3.3.**

3. Save the file and load it in your browser. The result should resemble **Figure 3.6.**

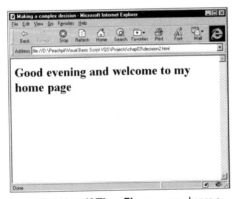

Figure 3.6 Using **If-Then-Else,** you can change a heading or message based on the time of day or the date. This sort of decision making can come in handy when you want to make your pages seem a little more lively.

```
If condition Then
    VBScript statements
Else
    VBScript statements
End If
```

Figure 3.4 The **Else** code only executes the condition isn't met.

```
If condition Then
    VBScript statements
ElseIf
    VBScript statements
Else
    VBScript statements
End If
```

Figure 3.5 An **ElseIf** clause lets you "nest" together **if** statements.

Script 3.3 **If-Then** statements can create similar results, but **If-Then-ElseIf** is more efficient.

```
File  Edit  Search  Help

<HTML>
<HEAD><TITLE>More decisions</TITLE></HEAD>
<BODY BGCOLOR="#FFFFFF">

<SCRIPT LANGUAGE="VBSCRIPT">
<!--
  Dim theDate

  theDate = WeekDay(Today)

  Document.Write "Today is " &
MonthName(Month(Today)) & " " & theDate & "<P>"

  If Hour(Time) <= 12 Then
      Document.Write "<H1>Good morning "
  ElseIf Hour(Time) <= 18 Then
      Document.Write "<H1>Good afternoon "
  Else
      Document.Write "<H1>Good evening "
  End If
  Document.Write " and welcome to my home
page</H1>"
-->
</SCRIPT>
</BODY>
</HTML>
```

Select Case expression

  Case first case

    VBScript statements

  Case other cases...

Case Else

    VBScript statements

End Select

Figure 3.7 Each **Case** part represents a value the expression can equal. If the expression doesn't match any of the cases, **Case Else** handles the outcome.

Script 3.4 Create messages for each month.

```
File  Edit  Search  Help

<HTML>
<HEAD><TITLE>More decisions</TITLE></HEAD>
<BODY BGCOLOR="#FFFFFF">

<SCRIPT LANGUAGE="VBSCRIPT">
<!--
  Document.Write "It's " & MonthName(Month(Date)) &
"...<BR>"
  Select Case MonthName(Month(Date))
    Case "January"
      Document.Write "The coldest month of all"
    Case "February"
      Document.Write "Be my valentine"
    Case "March"
      Document.Write "Beware the Ides of March"
    Case "April"
      Document.Write "April Fools!"
    Case "May"
      Document.Write "Ring around the rosey..."
    Case "June"
      Document.Write "Beaver, give Wally back his hat!"
    Case "July"
      Document.Write "Celebrate the fourth of July"
    Case "August"
      Document.Write "It's the Windows 95 Anniversary"
    Case "September"
      Document.Write "Back to School"
    Case "October"
      Document.Write "Happy Halloween"
    Case "November"
      Document.Write "Happy Thanksgiving"
    Case "December"
      Document.Write "Happy Holidays"
  End Select
-->
</SCRIPT>
</BODY>
</HTML>
```

CASE BY CASE DECISIONS

VBScript provides one other decision-making structure, **Select Case**. This structure allows you to consider a number of possible outcomes and respond accordingly. A **Select Case** block looks something like **Figure 3.7**.

Use **Select Case** when you have a large list of possible outcomes. If the expression doesn't ever match one of the cases, you can handle that outcome with **Case Else**.

To use Select Case:

1. Create a new HTML file and save it as select.html

2. Enter code inside the body section, as shown in **Script 3.4.**

3. Now, save the file and load it in your browser. You will get a special message that is tailored to the current month, as shown in **Figure 3.8.**

Tips:

- Remember, all of the code from this book can be found at

  http://www.internet-nexus.com/vbvqs

- For more information about the built-in time and date functions like **MonthName**, **Month** and **Date**, check out Chapter 2.

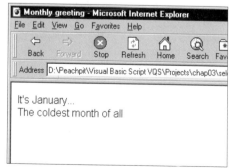

Figure 3.8 Use VBScript to display special messages or quotes that are relevant to the time of year.

USING LOOPS

Loops repeat VBScript statements until a condition is met. This may be when a condition is true or when it is false. VBScript provides four types of looping structures, shown in **Table 3.2.** When the condition is met, normal, sequential script execution continues.

Do-Until is the simplest kind of loop. It can take two forms, as shown in **Figure 3.9** and **Figure 3.10.**

To create a Do-Until loop:

1. Create a blank HTML file and save it as loop.html

2. Add a script section inside the body, as shown in **Script 3.5.**

3. Save the file and load it in your browser. The result should resemble **Figure 3.11.**

Table 3.2 The four kinds of loop.

LOOP	WHAT IT DOES
Do-Until	repeats until a condition is met
Do-While	repeats while a condition exists
While-Wend	repeats while a condition is exists
For-Next	makes a decision with a long list of possible outcomes

```
Do

    VBScript statements

Until condition
```

Figure 3.9 Do-Until is the simplest kind of loop.

```
Do Until condition

    VBScript statements

Loop
```

Figure 3.10 In this type of **Do-Until** loop, the loop may not ever execute, because the condition may be met the first time around. If this happens the whole loop is skipped.

```
1 2 3 4 5 6 7 8 9 10
```

Figure 3.11 This **Do-Until** loop that displays the numbers 1 through 10.

Script 3.5 Loops are scripts that occur repeatedly until a condition is met.

```
File  Edit  Search  Help
<HTML>
<HEAD><TITLE>Simple loops</TITLE></HEAD>
<BODY BGCOLOR="#FFFFFF">

<SCRIPT LANGUAGE="VBSCRIPT">
<!--
    Dim Counter

    Counter = 1
    Do
        Document.Write Counter & " "
        Counter = Counter + 1
    Loop Until Counter > 10
-->
</SCRIPT>
</BODY>
</HTML>
```

```
Do While condition

  VBScript statements

Loop
```

Figure 3.12 In the first form of the **Do-While** loop, the VBScript statements may ever execute because the condition may be met the first time it occurs.

```
Do

  VBScript statements

While condition
```

Figure 3.13 In the second form, the loop will always execute at least once because the condition isn't tested until the loop is over.

Script 3.6 You can use **Do-While** to create borders with text characters.

```
File  Edit  Search  Help

<HTML>
<HEAD><TITLE>Do While loops</TITLE></HEAD>
<BODY BGCOLOR="#FFFFFF">

<SCRIPT LANGUAGE="VBSCRIPT">
<!--
  Dim Count
  Document.Write "<CENTER><H1>Welcome to my Home
Page</H1>"
  Count = 1
  Do
    Document.Write "*"
    Count = Count + 1
  Loop While Count <= 60
  Document.Write "<H3>The home of Elvis on the
Net!</H3>"
  Count = 1
  Do
    Document.Write "*"
    Count = Count + 1
  Loop While Count <= 60
-->
</SCRIPT>
</BODY>
</HTML>
```

CREATING LOOPS WITH DO-WHILE

The **Do-While** loop is the opposite of the Do-Until; it repeats a block of code while a condition is met. If the condition is true, the block of code repeats. If it is not, script execution moves on to the line of code after the loop. Do-While has two forms, as shown in **Figure 3.12** and **Figure 3.13**.

To use the Do-While loop:

1. Create an empty HTML file and save it as while.html

2. Add a script section inside the body, as shown in **Script 3.6**.

3. Save the file and view it in your browser. The result should resemble **Figure 3.14**.

Tip:

- Notice the subtle difference between the two **Do-While** loops shown and the two equivalent **Do-Until** loops shown in the previous section. With **Do-While**, the condition doesn't have to change when you switch between forms. When you use **Do-Until**, however, the condition is different for each form. This may make **Do-While** a little easier to use.

Figure 3.14 Do-While loops allow you to easily output repeating characters.

CREATING LOOPS WITH WHILE-WEND

The While-Wend loop repeatedly executes a block of code as long as a condition is true. When the condition becomes false, the execution of script codes jumps to the first line of code after the loop. **Figure 3.15** shows what a While-Wend loop looks like.

The While-Wend loop doesn't offer any advantages over the Do-While loop. In general, you are better off using a Do-While instead.

To use a While-Wend loop:

1. Create an empty HTML file and save it as wend.html

2. Add a script section inside the body, as shown in **Script 3.7.**

3. Save the file and view it in your browser. Your result should resemble **Figure 3.16.**

```
While condition

    VBScript statements

Wend
```

Figure 3.15 A typical **While-Wend** loop will look very similar to a **Do-While** loop.

Script 3.7 This script calls the ASCII character set and prints it to the screen.

```
File  Edit  Search  Help

<HTML>
<HEAD><TITLE>While Wend loops</TITLE></HEAD>
<BODY BGCOLOR="#FFFFFF">

<SCRIPT LANGUAGE="VBSCRIPT">
<!--
    Dim MyCharacter

    MyCharacter = Chr(0)
    While MyCharacter <> "["
        Document.Write MyCharacter & " "
        MyCharacter = Chr(Asc(MyCharacter) + 1)
    Wend
-->
</SCRIPT>
</BODY>
</HTML>
```

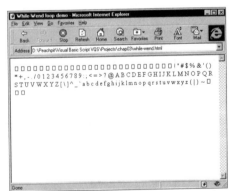

Figure 3.16 The ASCII character set courtesy of **While-Wend.**

```
For counter = start value
To end value Step step
value

    VBScript statements

    Exit For

    VBScript statements

Next
```

Figure 3.17 The **For-Next** loop uses the counter, start, end, and step values to determine how many times it will loop through the code block it contains.

```
For x = 1 to 10

    Document.Write x & " "

Next
```

Figure 3.18 A simple **For-Next** loop.

```
For x = 0 to 100 Step 10

    Document.Write x & " "

Next
```

Figure 3.19 Here's a simple **For-Next** loop that uses Step to count to one hundred in increments of ten.

```
For x = 10 to 1 Step -1

    Document.Write x & " "

Next
```

Figure 3.20 This **For-Next** loop counts backwards.

USING FOR-NEXT LOOPS

The final looping construct we will discuss in this chapter is the most famous. **For-Next** uses a counter value that is incremented each time the loop repeats. **Figure 3.17** shows the basic form of a **For-Next** loop. **Figure 3.18** shows a simple example.

For-Next is more powerful than other types of loops, and its beauty lies in the many ways it can be used. Using the optional **Step** part, you can determine how the loop increments, as shown in **Figure 3.19**. **For-Next** can even count backwards, as shown in **Figure 3.20.** This example counts from ten down to one.

Finally, **For-Next** supports a way to break out of the loop early, as shown in **Figure 3.21.** The optional **Exit For** is very similar to the **Exit Do** offered by the **Do-Until** and **Do-While** loops.

Though **For-Next** seems complicated at first, it is the best general-purpose looping construct that VBScript offers. It is also the one you are most likely to see in other people's scripting code on the Net.

(*Continued on the next page.*)

```
For x = 100 to 200 Step 10

    If x = 170 Then

        Exit For

    End If

    Document.Write x & " "

Next
```

Figure 3.21 This **For-Next** loop uses **Exit For** to break out of the loop early.

(Continued from the previous page.)

To use the For-Next loop:

1. Create a blank HTML file and save it as fornext.html

2. Add a script section above the body section, as shown in **Script 3.8.**

3. Add a script section inside of the body section, as shown in **Script 3.9.**

4. Save the file and load it into your browser. The result should resemble **Figure 3.22.**

Script 3.9 This script repeatedly calls the **For Next** procedure called **Movie_Rating** and passes that procedure a different movie each time.

```
File  Edit  Search  Help

<HTML>
<HEAD><TITLE>Using For Next</TITLE></HEAD>

<SCRIPT LANGUAGE="VBSCRIPT">
<!--
  Sub Movie_Rating (Num)
    Dim Count
    For Count = 1 to Num
      Document.Write "*"
    Next
  End Sub
-->
</SCRIPT>
<BODY BGCOLOR="#FFFFFF">

<SCRIPT LANGUAGE="VBSCRIPT">
<!--
  Document.Write "<H1>My Sci-Fi Movie
Reviews</H1>"

  Document.Write "<H3>Star Wars</H3>"
  Call Movie_Rating(5)

  Document.Write "<H3>Independence Day</H3>"
  Call Movie_Rating(3)

  Document.Write "<H3>Aliens</H3>"
  Call Movie_Rating(5)

  Document.Write "<H3>Jurassic Park</H3>"
  Call Movie_Rating(4)

  Document.Write "<H3>2010</H3>"
  Call Movie_Rating(2)

-->
</SCRIPT>
</BODY>
</HTML>
```

Script 3.8 The procedure called **Movie_Rating** uses a **For-Next** loop to print out a number of stars, based on the number that is passed to it.

```
File  Edit  Search  Help

<HTML>
<HEAD><TITLE>Using For Next</TITLE></HEAD>

<SCRIPT LANGUAGE="VBSCRIPT">
<!--
  Sub Movie_Rating (Num)
    Dim Count
    For Count = 1 to Num
      Document.Write "*"
    Next
  End Sub
-->
</SCRIPT>
<BODY BGCOLOR="#FFFFFF">
</BODY>
</HTML>
```

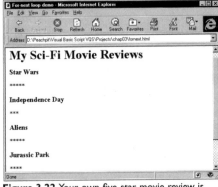

Figure 3.22 Your own five-star movie review is made possible with the **For-Next** loop.

OBJECTS AND EVENTS

This is where the fun really starts. The *objects* you use in VBScript are among the most powerful features of the language. Programmers love talking about objects, so you might think that this chapter is going to be rather complicated. Actually, objects are one of the simplest concepts you'll ever learn.

Consider the automobile. We can accept that the word *automobile* describes a type of thing. When you read the word *automobile*, you understand what it means immediately. An automobile is an object. A generic object, certainly, but that's the point. There are even more specific objects, like Oldsmobiles and Hondas. An actual Honda, the one you might drive around, is an *instance* of a Honda object. It is the thing you can see, touch, and use. It helps to think of things in terms of objects and instances when you're scripting Web pages.

While it is possible to create your own objects in VBScript, and create instances of those objects, you will typically use the objects that are built into the language. These built-in objects are known collectively as *the ActiveX Scripting Object Model*. It sounds complicated, but this object model—simply a collection of built-in objects you can use and abuse—is one of the biggest reasons to use VBScript. Let's take a look.

OF OBJECTS AND HIERARCHIES

Hierarchy is another one of those technical-sounding words that actually describes something relatively simple. The hierarchy in the object model consists of objects in the Web browser, as shown in **Figure 4.1.**

These objects represent specific things in the browser. Some of them may be obvious: the Document object, for instance, represents the document that is currently loaded in the browser. In fact, to VBScript the current document is an instance of the Document object. Other objects, like the Navigator and Location objects, may not be obvious, but you will learn about all of these objects in detail in the next three chapters. **Table 4.1** provides a quick explanation of the objects.

All objects have characteristics that make them unique. In VBScript, objects have three ways to differentiate themselves, with properties, methods, and events. A *property* is a list of characteristics. All objects in the object model have at least one property. Most objects can perform some sort of action. This occurs in a special function called a method. A *method* is simply a function that is tied to a specific object. Finally, objects can respond to *events*. You are probably familiar with events and event handling from our exploration of the subject in Chapter 2. The next few sections discuss object properties, methods, and events.

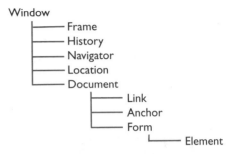

Figure 4.1 In the object model, the **Window** object sits at the top and contains all of the other objects. This is similar to the way that a Cutlass Supreme contains the steering wheel and other objects. The **Document** object, which is a sub-object of **Window,** contains some objects as well. The **Form** object also contains yet another object, called **Element.**

Table 4.1 The Object Model Hierarchy

OBJECT	WHAT IT IS
Window	the actual browser window
Frame	a list of any frames contained by the browser window
History	the browser's list of Web pages the user visited recently
Navigator	information about the browser's application program
Location	information about the window's current URL
Document	the document currently loaded in the browser window
Link	a list of any hyperlinks that appear in the current document
Anchor	a list of any anchor elements found in the current document
Form	a list of any forms that appear in the current document
Element	a list of the form elements that appear in the current form

Figure 4.2 Dot notation is used to access an object's properties, in this case the **name** property of the **Window** object.

Script 4.1 Your blank HTML template.

```
File  Edit  Search  Help
<HTML>

<HEAD><TITLE>Accessing a property</TITLE></HEAD>

<BODY BGCOLOR="#FFFFFF">
<SCRIPT LANGUAGE="VBSCRIPT">
<!--

-->
</SCRIPT>
</BODY>

</HTML>
```

Script 4.2 This script accesses the **title** property of the document.

```
File  Edit  Search  Help
<HTML>

<HEAD><TITLE>Accessing a property</TITLE></HEAD>

<BODY BGCOLOR="#FFFFFF">
<SCRIPT LANGUAGE="VBSCRIPT">
<!--
Document.write "<P>The document title is <I>" &
Document.title & "</I>"
-->
</SCRIPT>
</BODY>

</HTML>
```

OBJECT PROPERTIES

Object properties are simply characteristics of the object. The Window object's name property describes the name of the current window. An object's name is a characteristic, just like a person's name is a characteristic. The more characteristics you know about any object, the more you know about that object.

Properties can generally be read and set. Object properties are stated using dot notation, as shown in **Figure 4.2**.

To use object properties:

1. Create a blank HTML document, as shown in **Script 4.1.** Save the file as proptest.html

2. Add the script section in the body of your file, as shown in **Script 4.2.**

3. Save the document and load it in your browser. Your result should resemble **Figure 4.3.**

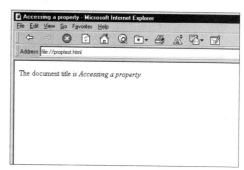

Figure 4.3 The title property of the **Document** object contains the title of the current document.

OBJECT METHODS

Methods are special built-in functions that work only with objects. One of the most commonly used object methods is the **Docu-ment** object's **write** method. You've been using this method a lot if you've been following along from the beginning of this book. The **write** method outputs a string of characters onto the current document. It accepts one parameter: the string of characters you wish to display.

To use object methods:

1. Create a blank HTML document and save the file as methodtest.html

2. Add a script section in the body, as shown in **Script 4.3**.

3. Save the document and load it in your browser. Your result should resemble **Figure 4.5**.

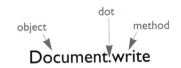

Figure 4.4 To an object, the method represents an action that the object can perform.

Script 4.3 The **Write** method allows you to include formatting along with your text string.

```
<HTML>
<HEAD><TITLE>Methods</TITLE></HEAD>

<BODY BGCOLOR="#FFFFFF">

<SCRIPT LANGUAGE="VBSCRIPT">
<!--
Document.write "<FONT SIZE=5>Welcome to my
VBScript page</FONT>"
Document.write "Here you will learn all of my
secrets."
Document.write "Prepare for Warp speed."
-->
</SCRIPT>
</BODY>
</HTML>
```

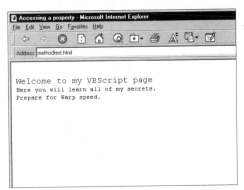

Figure 4.5 The **Document** object's **writeLn** method will output any text string.

OBJECT METHODS

Script 4.4 The **EVENT** and **FOR** attributes in the **<SCRIPT>** tag let the browser know to skip that code when the page loads and execute it only when the event identified by the **EVENT** attribute is triggered. In this case the event is clicking **Button1**.

```
File  Edit  Search  Help

<HTML>
<HEAD><TITLE>Script Section Event
Handler</TITLE>
</HEAD>

<BODY BGCOLOR="#FFFFFF">

<SCRIPT LANGUAGE="VBScript" EVENT="OnClick"
FOR="Button1">
<!--
    MsgBox "Hello, world!"
-->
</SCRIPT>

</BODY>
<HTML>
```

Script 4.5 VBScript comes with a number of built-in buttons and boxes, which are introduced in Chapter 2.

```
File  Edit  Search  Help

<HTML>
<HEAD><TITLE>Script Section Event
Handler</TITLE>
</HEAD>

<BODY BGCOLOR="#FFFFFF">

<SCRIPT LANGUAGE="VBScript" EVENT="OnClick"
FOR="Button1">
<!--
    MsgBox "Hello, world!"
-->
</SCRIPT>

<FORM>
  <INPUT TYPE=Button NAME=Button1
VALUE="Click me!">
</FORM>

</BODY>

</HTML>
```

HANDLING EVENTS

Events are the things that happen as a user travels through your site. Pages loading and closing, buttons being clicked—these are all events. In programming your Web page to react to an event in a certain way, you are *handling* an event.

An *object event* is something that happens to the object. The code that you use to handle an event is called an *event handler*. The name of the events always start with **on**.

There are three ways to handle most events with VBScript, as shown in the following sections: a dedicated script section, inline, or with a subroutine.

To handle an event with a script section:

1. Create a file with a script section as shown in **Script 4.4**. Save the file as event1.html

2. Create a form button called *click me* by adding code in the body section, as shown in **Script 4.5**

3. Load the page in your browser and click the button. The result should resemble **Figure 4.6**.

(Continued on the next page.)

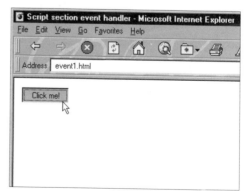

Figure 4.6 The user triggers an event by clicking the form button.

(Continued from the previous page.)

There is no logical limit to the number of events you can handle. To add another Form button to this page, for example, you can simply add another event handler to handle the event that occurs when that button is clicked.

To create multiple buttons that handle the click event:

1. Edit event1.html as shown in **Script 4.6** and save it as event2.html

2. Load the page in your browser. Notice that clicking each button triggers a separate event handler, as shown in **Figure 4.8.**

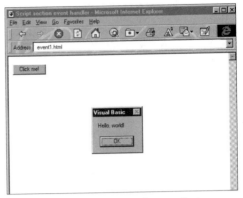

Figure 4.7 Running the page in Internet Explorer.

Figure 4.8 Each button opens a separate message box.

Script 4.6 You can add multiple buttons and events in a single script by placing them one after another.

```
<HTML>
<HEAD><TITLE>Script Section Event
Handler</TITLE></HEAD>

<BODY BGCOLOR="#FFFFFF">

<SCRIPT LANGUAGE="VBScript" EVENT="OnClick"
FOR="Button1">
<!--
    MsgBox "You clicked button1!"
-->
</SCRIPT>

<SCRIPT LANGUAGE="VBScript" EVENT="OnClick"
FOR="Button2">
<!--
    MsgBox "You clicked button2"
-->
</SCRIPT>

<FORM>
    <INPUT TYPE=Button NAME=Button1 VALUE="Click
me">
</FORM>

<FORM>
    <INPUT TYPE=Button NAME=Button2
VALUE="No, click me">
</FORM>

</BODY>
</HTML>
```

HANDLING EVENTS

Script 4.7 Inline event handlers are a good alternative if you are handling a lot of events. They take up very little space and save you a lot of typing.

```
File  Edit  Search  Help

<HTML>
<HEAD><TITLE>inline script event handler</TITLE>
</HEAD>

<BODY BGCOLOR="#FFFFFF">

<SCRIPT LANGUAGE="VBScript">
<!--
-->
</SCRIPT>

<FORM>
   <INPUT NAME="Button1" TYPE="BUTTON"
VALUE="Click me!" Onclick='MsgBox "Hello, world!"'>
</FORM>

</BODY>
</HTML>
```

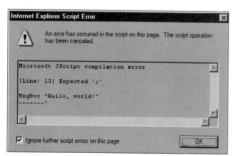

Figure 4.9 Internet Explorer will think you're using JScript inline unless you tell it otherwise.

CREATING AN INLINE EVENT HANDLER

VBScript allows you to add event-handling code as an inline attribute in HTML tags, which can be useful if you have a lot of events to handle. Using this method, you add an **OnClick** attribute to the <INPUT> tag, which makes a separate script section unnecessary.

To create an inline event handler:

1. Create a file with the code shown in **Script 4.7.** Save it as **event4.html**

2. Load the page in your browser and click the button.

Internet Explorer bug:

■ You might have noticed the empty VBScript script section in the HTML code you just entered. This empty code block shouldn't be necessary, but it seems that Internet Explorer defaults to JScript, Microsoft's version of JavaScript, if you don't specify a script language before using inline code. The inline code you entered is not very good JScript code as it turns out, and Internet Explorer will squawk if you try to use it without a VBScript script section somewhere in the document, even an empty one.

HANDLING EVENTS WITH SUBROUTINES

Procedures allow you to organize event-handling code in a more logical and readable fashion. A procedure event handler looks something like **Script 4.8.** For a refresher on subroutines, check out Chapter 2.

To handle events with subroutines:

1. Create an empty HTML file. Save the file as event3.html

2. Add two alert buttons to the page, in the body section, as shown in **Script 4.9.**

3. Add a script block with the event handlers before the body section, as shown in **Script 4.10.**

4. Save the file and load it in your browser. When you click the button, the message box appears, as shown in **Figure 4.10.**

Tip:

- Events are intimately involved with objects. Subsequent chapters in this book cover the objects, and their related events.

Script 4.8 In this prototype code, **<OBJECT>** represents the name of the object to which the event occurs. This can be a built-in object or an object you created yourself.

```
File  Edit  Search  Help
<HTML>
<HEAD><TITLE>Events with subroutines</TITLE></HEAD>
<SCRIPT LANGUAGE="VBSCRIPT">
<!--
   Sub <Object>_On<Event>
      VBScript code to handle the event goes here
   End Sub
-->
</SCRIPT>
```

Script 4.9 Add two built-in alert boxes. To learn more about built-in functions, see Chapter 2.

```
File  Edit  Search  Help
<HTML>
<HEAD><TITLE>Events with subroutines</TITLE></HEAD>
<SCRIPT LANGUAGE="VBSCRIPT">
<!--
   Sub DisplayHello()
      Alert "Hoochie Goochie!"
   End Sub

   Sub DisplayGoodbye()
      Alert "Leaving so soon?"
   End Sub
-->
</SCRIPT>

<BODY BGCOLOR="FFFFFF">
</BODY>
</HTML>
```

Script 4.10 You can place multiple events when working with subroutines, too.

```
File  Edit  Search  Help
   Sub DisplayGoodbye()
      Alert "Leaving so soon?"
   End Sub
-->
</SCRIPT>
<SCRIPT LANGUAGE="VBSCRIPT">
<!--
      onLoad = "DisplayHello()"
      onUnload = "DisplayGoodbye()" >
-->
</SCRIPT>

<BODY BGCOLOR="FFFFFF">
</BODY>
</HTML>
```

Figure 4.10 You can write your own procedures to handle events.

Controlling the Browser Window

5

Window
├── Frame
├── History
├── Navigator
├── Location
└── Document
    ├── Link
    ├── Anchor
    └── Form
        └── Element

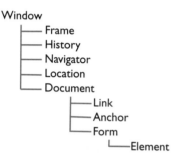

Figure 5.1 In the object model hierarchy, the **Window** object sits at the top and contains all of the other objects.

The **Window** object gives you control over the one thing that the user looks at again and again—the browser. This chapter shows you how to use the **Window** object to control the browser window and how to add functionality that will make your pages more compelling.

The **Window** object sits at the top of the object model hierarchy and contains several sub-objects: the **Frame, Navigator, Location,** and **Document** objects. Because it sits at the top of this hierarchy, it is available to use at all times: you can use **Window** object properties, methods, and events without using the keyword **Window** in your script. For example, the following lines of script are identical:

> Window.alert "Help, I've fallen and I can't get up!"
>
> alert "Help, I've fallen and I can't get up!"

The **Window** object has several properties and methods, plus two events. In the following pages, you will take a quick look at these attributes. If you need a refresher on using objects and their properties, methods, and events, please refer to Chapter 4.

WINDOW PROPERTIES, METHODS, AND EVENTS

The Window object introduces the properties shown in **Table 5.1.** Many of them, like docu-ment, history, location, and navigator, simply refer to other objects contained by the current window. For example, the **Document** object has a **write** method that you may recognize:

    Document.write "Hello, world!"

When you want to access the **write** method through the **Window** object's document property, you can use an extended form of dot notation:

    Window.document.write "Hello, world!"

In this case, you are accessing the same method in a slightly different way. The Win-dow object has a property called **document.** This **document** property is itself a **Document** object that has a **write** property.

The Window object introduces the methods shown in **Table 5.2.** Many of these methods, like **alert** and **confirm,** open new windows or dialog boxes. Remember that methods are nothing more than functions that are tied to a particular object.

The **Window** object uses only two events, **onLoad** and **onUnload.** I bet you can guess what they do (don't cheat by looking at **Table 5.3** either!). If you need to execute scripting code when the window opens and closes, this is the place to go.

Table 5.1 The properties of the **Window** object.

PROPERTY	WHAT IT IS
defaultStatus	the default text that will appear in the current window's status bar
document	the Document object for the current window
frames	the list of frames for the current window
history	the History object for the current window
location	the Location object for the current window
name	the name of the current window
navigator	the Navigator object for the current window
opener	the Window object that opened the current window
parent	the frame that contains the current window
self	the current window's Window object
status	used to set the text in the current window's status bar
top	the Window object that is the topmost window

Table 5.2 The methods of the **Window** object.

METHOD	WHAT IT IS
alert	displays a dialog box with an alert method
clearTimeout	clears a particular timer
close	closes the current browser window
confirm	displays a dialog box with OK and Cancel choices
navigate	navigates the window to a new URL
open	opens a new browser window
prompt	prompts the user for input
setTimeout	calls a function after a period of time has elapsed

Table 5.3 The events of the **Window** object.

EVENT	OCCURS WHEN
onLoad	occurs when the page in the window fully loads
onUnload	occurs when the page in the window closes

> Window.defaultStatus = "Welcome to
> my Web page!"

Figure 5.2 The defaultStatus property lets you display messages in the browser's status bar. **Figure 5.3** shows what this looks like in the browser window.

Figure 5.3 The status bar message is at the bottom left of the browser window.

Script 5.1 The empty HTML file for your project.

```
File  Edit  Search  Help
<HTML>
<HEAD><TITLE>Using the defaultStatus
property</TITLE></HEAD>

<BODY BGCOLOR="#FFFFFF">

</BODY>
</HTML>
```

Script 5.2 It's best to place this code near the beginning of your page, so that it will be the first thing the browser does.

```
File  Edit  Search  Help
<HTML>
<HEAD><TITLE>Using the defaultStatus
property</TITLE></HEAD>

<SCRIPT LANGUAGE="VBSCRIPT">
<!--
  Sub Window_onLoad
    defaultStatus = "Eat at Alice's
restaurant!"
  End Sub
-->
</SCRIPT>

<BODY BGCOLOR="#FFFFFF">

</BODY>
</HTML>
```

CUSTOMIZING THE STATUS BAR

The **defaultStatus** property determines the text that appears by default in the browser's status bar. This text string displays there unless another object overwrites it. In your code, **defaultStatus** looks like **Figure 5.2.** You can place this property in the event handler for the **Window** object's **onLoad** event, which runs when the window first loads, as shown in the following steps.

To set default text for the status bar:

1. Create a new HTML file that resembles **Script 5.1.** Save the file as **dstatus.html**

2. Add a script section above the body, as shown in **Script 5.2.**

3. Save the file and load it in your browser. Your result should resemble **Figure 5.4.**

Tips:

- A good place to use the **defaultStatus** property is in the event handler for the Windows object's **onLoad** event.

- By handling the **onLoad** event of the **Window** object, you ensure that the default status bar text is displayed when the window first opens.

- It is possible to change the status bar text at other times, say, in response to an event.

Figure 5.4 The status bar message is up to you: it can be added to any Web page.

CHANGING THE STATUS BAR

Setting the default status bar message with the **defaultStatus** property is nice, but you may want to change the text that appears in the status bar often, say in response to an event. To do so, just use **status** on its own. By handling the **onLoad** event of the Window object, you ensure that the status bar text displays when the window first opens.

To change the status bar text:

1. Create a new HTML file, or open an existing one. Save the file as **cstatus.html**

2. Add a script section above the body, as shown in **Script 5.3.**

3. Save the file and load it in your browser. Your result should resemble **Figure 5.5.**

Script 5.3 Using a string like **Windows.status** allows you to customize the status bar on each page you create.

```
 File  Edit  Search  Help

<HTML>
<HEAD><TITLE>Using the status
property</TITLE></HEAD>

<SCRIPT LANGUAGE="VBSCRIPT">
<!--
    Sub Window_onLoad
        Window.status = "Welcome to Pizzeria Bianco!"
    End Sub
-->
</SCRIPT>

<BODY BGCOLOR="#FFFFFF">

</BODY>
</HTML>
```

Welcome to Pizzeria Bianco!

Figure 5.5 The **Window** object provides a **status** property that lets you change the text in the status bar at the bottom of the browser window at any time.

```
<A HREF="http://www.bigtent.com"
NAME="lnkBigTent">Big Tent</A>
```

Figure 5.6 To access a hyperlink in VBScript, you simply have to give it a name. In this case, the named link, **lnkBigTent,** is an instance of the link object. For a refresher on objects and instances of objects, check out Chapter 4.

Script 5.4 This code adds four hyperlinks to the page, each with a unique name. Each one is a unique instance of the **Link** object.

```
File  Edit  Search  Help
<HTML>
<HEAD><TITLE>Using link object</TITLE></HEAD>

<BODY BGCOLOR="#FFFFFF">

<B>Nav Menu</B>
<BR><A HREF="http://www.bigtent.com"
NAME="aBigTent">
    Big Tent Media Labs</A>

<BR><A HREF="http://www.hipmama.com"
NAME="aHipMama">
    Hip Mama</A>

<BR><A HREF="http://www.internet-nexus.com"
NAME="aNexus">
    Internet Nexus</A>

<BR><A HREF="http://www.lofy.com" NAME="aLOFY">
    Looking Out For Yourself</A>

</BODY>
</HTML>
```

DESCRIBING LINKS IN THE STATUS BAR

The **status** property opens up interesting possibilities when used with some of the other objects in the object model hierarchy. Using the **Link** object, for example, you can change the status bar as the mouse pointer passes over a hyperlink. This is a great way to provide people who use your site with valuable information about where they can go and what they can do. To do this, you must first create a list of links and then introduce the text that will appear when the mouse passes over them.

To create a list of links:

1. Create a blank HTML file and name it **status.html**

2. Add the code in the body section, as shown in **Script 5.4.**

You can now handle the **onMouseOver** event for each hyperlink to display a text message in the status bar.

(*Continued on the next page.*)

(Continued from the previous page.)

To create a message that describes each link:

1. Open **status.html** if it isn't already open.

2. Create a script section above the body, as shown in **Script 5.5**.

3. Save the file and load it in your browser. Your result should resemble **Figure 5.7**.

Tip:

- Some of these code statements can get pretty long. To save yourself some time, and avoid making typing errors, you can copy all of these code examples from

  http://www.internet-nexus/vbvqs

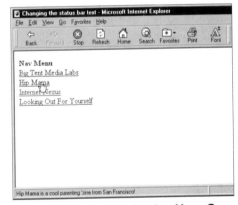

Figure 5.7 Using the **Link** object's **onMouseOver** event with the **Window** object's **status** property helps you add features that make your pages more user-friendly.

Script 5.5 This code creates an **onMouseOver** event for each of the objects. A special message describing each link appears in the status bar, as shown in **Figure 5.7**.

```
File  Edit  Search  Help

<HTML>
<HEAD><TITLE>Using link object</TITLE></HEAD>

<SCRIPT LANGUAGE="VBSCRIPT">
<!--
  Sub aBigTent_onMouseOver
    Window.status = "Big Tent Media Labs is a
publishing company specializing in twingling!"
  End Sub

  Sub aHipMama_onMouseOver
    Window.status = "Hip Mama is a cool
parenting 'zine from San Francisco!"
  End Sub

  Sub aNexus_onMouseOver
    Window.status = "The Internet Nexus is the
home of WinInfo, your source for Windows news
and information!"
  End Sub

  Sub aLOFY_onMouseOver
    Window.status = "Looking Out For Yourself
gives you a place to turn in troubled times"
  End Sub
-->
</SCRIPT>

<BODY BGCOLOR="#FFFFFF">

<B>Nav Menu</B>
<BR><A HREF="http://www.bigtent.com"
NAME="aBigTent">
    Big Tent Media Labs</A>

<BR><A HREF="http://www.hipmama.com"
NAME="aHipMama">
    Hip Mama</A>

<BR><A HREF="http://www.internet-nexus.com"
NAME="aNexus">
    Internet Nexus</A>

<BR><A HREF="http://www.lofy.com" NAME="aLOFY">
    Looking Out For Yourself</A>

</BODY>
</HTML>
```

Script 5.6 This script adds three form buttons that will act as a navigational toolbar.

```
File  Edit  Search  Help
<HTML>
<HEAD><TITLE>Using the navigate
method</TITLE></HEAD>

<BODY BGCOLOR="#FFFFFF">

<FORM NAME="Form1"><B>Nav Menu</B>
   <BR><INPUT TYPE="Button" NAME="btnMicrosoft"
VALUE="Microsoft">
   <BR><INPUT TYPE="Button" NAME="btnApple"
VALUE="Apple">
   <BR><INPUT TYPE="Button" NAME="btnNetscape"
VALUE="Netscape">
</FORM>

</BODY>
</HTML>
```

Script 5.7 The completed **navigate.html** file.

```
File  Edit  Search  Help
<HTML>
<HEAD><TITLE>Using the navigate
method/TITLE></HEAD>

<SCRIPT LANGUAGE="VBSCRIPT">
<!--
   Sub btnMicrosoft_onClick
      Navigate("http://www.microsoft.com")
   End Sub

   Sub btnApple_onClick
      Navigate("http://www.apple.com")
   End Sub

   Sub btnNetscape_onClick
      Navigate("http://home.netscape.com")
   End Sub
-->
</SCRIPT>

<BODY BGCOLOR="#FFFFFF">

<FORM NAME="Form1"><B>Nav Menu</B>
   <BR><INPUT TYPE="Button" NAME="btnMicrosoft""
VALUE="Microsoft">
   <BR><INPUT TYPE="Button" NAME="btnApple"
VALUE="Apple">
   <BR><INPUT TYPE="Button" NAME="btnNetscape"
VALUE="Netscape">
</FORM>

</BODY>
</HTML>
```

JUMPING TO A NEW LOCATION

Often, you will want the browser to jump to a new location in response to a user's action, say clicking a button or an image. This can be accomplished with the **navigate** method of the **Window** object, which takes the browser to a new URL. The following code does just that:

    navigate("http://www.bigtent.com")

To create a menu of jump buttons:

1. Create a blank HTML file, and save it as navigate.html

2. Add code within the body section to add three form buttons to the page, as shown in **Script 5.6.**

Now, you must add event handlers to each of the buttons using VBScript.

3. Enter the script section above the body section, as shown in **Script 5.7.**

4. Save the file and load it into your browser. Your result should resemble **Figure 5.8.**

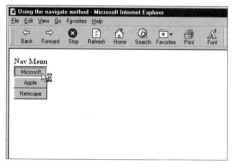

Figure 5.8 The event handlers will use the **navigate** method to cause the browser to jump to a new location each time the user clicks a button.

DISPLAYING BROWSER INFORMATION

The Window object contains many objects, among them navigator. The Navigator object itself has properties, shown in **Table 5.4** that call information about the browser onto your Web page.

To display information about the browser:

1. Create a blank HTML file and save it as navigator.html

2. Add a script above the body section, as shown in **Script 5.8.**

3. Save the file and load it in your browser. **Figure 5.9** shows the result.

To display multiple lines of information about the browser:

1. Create a blank HTML file and save it as navigator2.html

2. Add a script inside the body section, as shown in **Script 5.9.**

3. Save the file and load it in your browser. **Figure 5.10** shows the result.

Script 5.9 You can string together multiple properties with the **&** operator to show a list of information about the browser.

```
File  Edit  Search  Help
<HTML>
<HEAD><TITLE>Using all the properties of the
Navigator object</TITLE></HEAD>

<SCRIPT LANGUAGE="VBSCRIPT">
<!--
   Document.write(Navigator.appCodeName & "<BR>"
   & Navigator.appName & "<BR>" &
Navigator.appVersion & "<BR>" &
Navigator.userAgent)
-->
</SCRIPT>

<BODY BGCOLOR="#FFFFFF">

</BODY>
</HTML>
```

Table 5.4 The properties of the **Navigator** object.

PROPERTY	WHAT IT DOES
appCodeName	returns "Mozilla," the code name for Netscape Navigator 1.0
appName	returns the name of the Web browser
appVersion	returns the version of the browser and the user's operating system
userAgent	returns both the name and the version of the browser, as well as the user's operating system

Script 5.8 This code is an example of how to use the **Navigator** object. You can drop this code into any of your pages.

```
File  Edit  Search  Help
<HTML>
<HEAD><TITLE>Using the Navigator
object</TITLE></HEAD>

<SCRIPT LANGUAGE="VBSCRIPT">
<!--
   Document.write(Navigator.appName)
-->
</SCRIPT>

<BODY BGCOLOR="#FFFFFF">

</BODY>
</HTML>
```

Figure 5.9 Printing out the browser application name in Internet Explorer.

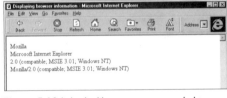

Figure 5.10 It looks like someone upgraded to Windows NT; here's all the browser info you can get with the **Navigator** object.

DISPLAYING BROWSER INFORMATION

Script 5.10 You can just drop this code into any existing file as well, changing the message as you wish.

```
File  Edit  Search  Help
<HTML>
<HEAD><TITLE>Displaying an alert dialog
box</TITLE></HEAD>

<SCRIPT LANGUAGE="VBSCRIPT">
<!--
  Sub Window_onLoad
    alert "Warning!  We have an important
message on the 'What's new' page. Please read
it immediately!"
  End Sub

-->
</SCRIPT>

<BODY BGCOLOR="#FFFFFF">

</BODY>
</HTML>
```

Figure 5.11 An alert dialog should only be used for important messages.

DISPLAYING AN ALERT DIALOG BOX

The **Window** object has an **alert** method that allows you to display a dialog box to the user. The code in its simplest form uses one parameter, and some text, which determines the message:

> alert ("Make sure you check out our recipe page!")

Generally, you only use an alert box to respond to something the user does. So the actual code always involves an event. In the following steps, you will create a page that displays an alert message when the window opens.

To display an alert dialog box when a page loads:

1. Create a blank HTML file and save it as alert.html

2. Add the script shown in **Script 5.10.**

3. Save the file and load it in your browser. **Figure 5.11** shows the result.

Tip:

■ Use the **alert** method with care: it's annoying to have dialog boxes popping up all over the place. If you absolutely must use an alert dialog, make sure you limit its use to responding to a user action or displaying very important information.

CREATING A PROMPT DIALOG BOX

A prompt dialog box collects information from your users through an edit field. Your VBScript code stores this text, and you can use this information to customize your page to your user. The **Window** object's prompt method makes all this possible. **Figure 5.12** shows its general form.

The following steps use a prompt dialog box to get the user's name.

To create a prompt dialog box:

1. Create a blank HTML file and save it as prompt.html

2. Add the script shown in **Script 5.11** within the body section.

3. Save the file and load it in your browser. **Figures 5.13** and **5.14** show the result.

Tips:

■ Create string values that relate to the content that they store. In **Script 5.11**, StrAge represents **Str**ing and **Age**.

■ The prompt dialog displays **<undefined>** if you don't specify a default value. If you want it to be empty, use an empty string (").

```
return string = prompt message, default
value
```

Figure 5.12 The **message** parameter determines what text will appear in the dialog box. The **default value** parameter sets a default value in the input box in the dialog box. When the user clicks OK, the value in the input box is sent back to the **return string** variable.

Script 5.11 You can name the **return string** whatever you like. It's a good idea to choose a descriptive name. This makes your code easy to read, understand, and edit over time.

```
File Edit Search Help
<HTML>
<HEAD><TITLE>Creating a prompt dialog
box</TITLE></HEAD>

<SCRIPT LANGUAGE="VBSCRIPT">
<!--
   strName = prompt("Please enter your first
name:", "")
   Document.write ("<H2> Hello, " & strName &
","")
   Document.write (" and welcome to this Web
page!</H2>")

-->
</SCRIPT>

<BODY BGCOLOR="#FFFFFF">

</BODY>
</HTML>
```

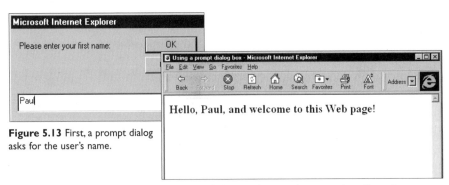

Figure 5.13 First, a prompt dialog asks for the user's name.

Figure 5.14 You can then use that name throughout the page.

Script 5.12 Create a form button.

```
File  Edit  Search  Help

<HTML>
<HEAD><TITLE>Closing the browser
window</TITLE></HEAD>

<BODY BGCOLOR="#FFFFFF">


<FORM>
  <INPUT NAME=Button1 TYPE=BUTTON VALUE="Close
the browser">
</FORM>

</BODY>
```

Script 5.13 Like some of the other properties, the close method needs to be triggered by an event, such as the click of a button.

```
File  Edit  Search  Help

<HTML>
<HEAD><TITLE>Closing the browser
window</TITLE></HEAD>

<SCRIPT LANGUAGE="VBSCRIPT">
<!--
  Sub Button1_onClick
    Close
  End Sub
-->
</SCRIPT>

<BODY BGCOLOR="#FFFFFF">


<FORM>
  <INPUT NAME=Button1 TYPE=BUTTON VALUE="Close
the browser">
</FORM>

</BODY>
```

CLOSING THE BROWSER WINDOW

The **Window** object has a method that lets you close the browser window. It is fairly easy to use. The following code will close the current browser window:

Close

It doesn't get any easier than that!

To close the browser window with a form button:

1. Create a new HTML file and save it as close.html

2. Add the code shown in **Script 5.12** to the body of the HTML file. This code creates the form button.

3. Now you need to add an event handler for the button's **onClick** event. This is done with the script section shown in **Script 5.13.**

4. Save the file and load it in your browser. **Figure 5.15** shows the result.

Note:

- Use the **close** method judiciously. The user can find it very annoying to have their window closed.

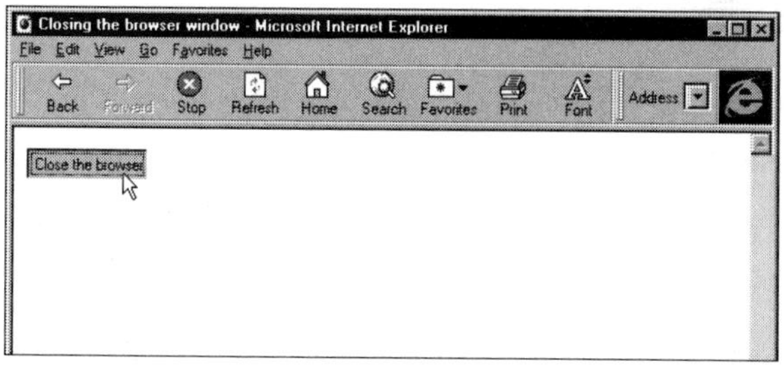

Figure 5.15 Click the button, and the browser window closes.

CONFIRMING A CHOICE

Sometimes you want to get the user's confirmation before you perform an action. Closing the browser window is a good example, as seen in the previous section. The Window object has a **confirm** method that does just that: it opens a dialog box that displays a message, an OK button, and a Cancel button. You can set the message to any valid VBScript text string and then execute code based on which button the user clicked.

The **confirm** method takes the form shown in **Figure 5.16.**

To offer a choice to close the browser window:

1. Create a new HTML file. Save it as confirm.html

2. Enter the code into the body to create a form button, as shown in **Script 5.14.**

3. Now, create an **onClick** event handler for the form button, as shown in **Script 5.15.**

4. Save the file and load it in your browser. Your result should resemble **Figure 5.17.**

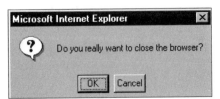

Figure 5.17 Put your users in charge and let them decide if they want to close the browser window.

---

return value = confirm(message string)

Figure 5.16 The **return value** tells you whether the user clicked OK or Cancel. The **message string** parameter is the text you want the dialog to display.

Script 5.14 This file is almost identical to the one in the previous section. If you completed that section, you may want to alter close.html, the file you created there.

```
File  Edit  Search  Help

<HTML>
<HEAD><TITLE>Confirming a choice</TITLE></HEAD>

<BODY BGCOLOR="#FFFFFF">

<FORM>
    <INPUT NAME=Button1 TYPE=BUTTON VALUE="Close
the browser">
</FORM>

</BODY>
</HTML>
```

Script 5.15 You can just drop this code into any existing file as well, changing the message as you wish.

```
File  Edit  Search  Help

<HTML>
<HEAD><TITLE>Confirming a choice</TITLE></HEAD>

<SCRIPT LANGUAGE="VBSCRIPT">
<!--
    Sub Button1_OnClick
        Ret = confirm("Do you really want to close
the browser?")
        If Ret = TRUE then close
    End Sub
-->
</SCRIPT>

<BODY BGCOLOR="#FFFFFF">

<FORM>
    <INPUT NAME=Button1 TYPE=BUTTON VALUE="Close
the browser">
</FORM>

</BODY>
</HTML>
```

```
open url, window_name, "toolbar=yes or
no, location=yes or no, directories=yes
or no, status=yes or no, menubar=yes or
no, scrollbars=yes or no, resizeable=yes
or no, width=pixels, height=pixels,
top=pixels, left=pixels"
```

Figure 5.18 The many parameters of the **open** method let you create new browser windows with whichever features you want. Horrible looking, isn't it? The good news is that most of the parameters are optional.

Script 5.16 Add a form button.

```
File  Edit  Search  Help
<HTML>
<HEAD><TITLE>Opening a new browser
window</TITLE></HEAD>

<BODY BGCOLOR="#FFFFFF">

<FORM>
  <INPUT NAME=Button1 TYPE=BUTTON VALUE="Open
second window">
</FORM>

</BODY>
</HTML>
```

Script 5.17 When you click on the button, a new window opens according to your specifications.

```
File  Edit  Search  Help
<HTML>
<HEAD><TITLE>Opening a new browser
window</TITLE></HEAD>

<SCRIPT LANGUAGE="VBSCRIPT">
<!--
  Sub Button1_onClick
        open "http://www.bigtent.com/index.html",
"window2","toolbar=no, menubar=no, width=640
height=480"
    End Sub
-->
</SCRIPT>

<BODY BGCOLOR="#FFFFFF">

<FORM>
  <INPUT NAME=Button1 TYPE=BUTTON VALUE="Open
second window">
</FORM>

</BODY>
</HTML>
```

OPENING A NEW BROWSER WINDOW

Just as you can close a browser window with **close**, you can create a new browser window with the **open** method. This method takes a dizzying array of parameters because of the number of optional features you might include in a browser window. **Figure 5.18** shows the general form of the **open** method.

The best way to understand the various parameters of the **open** method is to play around with them.

To open a new browser window:

1. Create a new HTML file and save it as open.html

2. Add code inside the body section, as shown in **Script 5.16**.

3. Now add a script section before the body section, as shown in **Script 5.17.**

4. Save the file and load it in your browser. When you click the button, the new window will open, as shown in **Figure 5.19.**

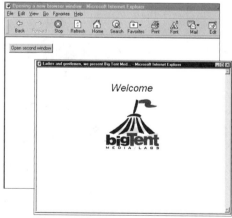

Figure 5.19 You can specify the attributes of the new window that you open using the **open** method.

USING ONLOAD AND onUnload EVENTS

The **Window** object has two events: **onLoad** and **onUnload**. They let you create events when users come and go from your Web pages. You can put the **onLoad** and **onUnload** events to work either within the body of your script code or as an event handler in a script section. For a refresher on events and event handlers, take a look at Chapter 4.

To use Onload and onUnload as a script section:

1. Create a new HTML file and save it as events.html

2. Add a script section above the body, as shown in **Script 5.18.**

3. Save the file and load it in your browser. When the page opens, an alert box appears, as shown in **Figure 5.20.**

To use Onload and onUnload as a body section:

1. Create a new HTML file and save it as events2.html

2. Add the body section, as shown in **Script 5.19.**

3. Save the file and load it in your browser. When the page opens, an alert box appears, as shown in **Figure 5.21.**

Figure 5.21 Using **onLoad** and **onUnload** events, you can prompt users as they come and go from your page.

Figure 5.20 The **onLoad** event allows you to execute script when the window first loads.

Script 5.18 This script section includes handlers for both the **onLoad** and **onUnload** events.

```
File  Edit  Search  Help

<HTML>
<HEAD><TITLE>Using OnLoad and
onUnload</TITLE></HEAD>

<SCRIPT LANGUAGE="VBSCRIPT">
<!--

   Sub Window_onLoad
     Window.status = "Welcome to my home page!"
   End Sub

   Sub Window_onUnload
     alert ("Thanks for visiting. Come by again
soon!")
   End Sub

-->
</SCRIPT>

<BODY BGCOLOR="#FFFFFF">
</BODY>
</HTML>
```

Script 5.19 This code creates the same effect as **Script 5.18.**

```
File  Edit  Search  Help

<HTML>
<HEAD><TITLE>Using OnLoad and
onUnload</TITLE></HEAD>

<BODY BGCOLOR="#FFFFFF">

<BODY onLoad="alert 'Welcome to my home page'"
onUnload="alert 'Thanks for visiting. Come by
again soon!'">

</BODY>
</HTML>
```

USING FRAMES

As you learn more about Web design, you will find yourself working with increasingly complex amounts of information. And soon enough, you'll find yourself wanting to know more about frames.

Frames are independent windows within the single browser window. A frames-based design divides a single browser window into independent areas called *framesets*. Each frame in a frameset is just like its own Web page. If you want some information, such as a navigation bar or a company logo, to always be at the top of your page, frames can be an elegant solution.

This chapter introduces frames and explains how to use VBScript to extend the things you do with HTML-based framesets.

CREATING A FRAMESET

You create frames with VBScript using the frames property of the Window object. While this isn't necessarily easier than creating frames in HTML, working with the VBScript version of frames is a good idea if you are using VBScript elsewhere in your pages.

To create a frameset:

1. Create a new HTML file and save it as simple.html

2. Enter the code shown in **Script 6.1** and save the file.

3. Create two blank files called blue.html and green. html

4. Load simple.html in your browser. The result should look like **Figure 6.1.**

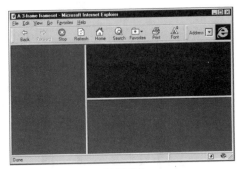

Figure 6.1 A standard HTML frameset.

Note:

■ Though blue.html and green.html are empty, they must exist for the frameset to appear. These files will ultimately contain content that appears in each of the different frames.

Script 6.1 This script creates a window that has three frames.

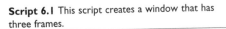

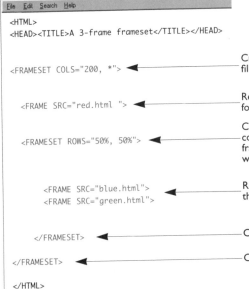

```
<HTML>
<HEAD><TITLE>A 3-frame frameset</TITLE></HEAD>

<FRAMESET COLS="200, *">     ◄——   Creates two columns: one is 200 pixels, the other
                                    fills the remainder of the browser window.

  <FRAME SRC="red.html ">    ◄——   Refers to another file that contains the content
                                    for the left-hand column.

  <FRAMESET ROWS="50%, 50%">  ◄——  Creates another frameset within the right-hand
                                    column. This code splits the column into two
                                    frames that each fill half of the available browser
                                    window.

    <FRAME SRC="blue.html">   ◄——   Refers to two files that contain the contents for
    <FRAME SRC="green.html">         the two frames in the right-hand column.

  </FRAMESET>                 ◄——   Closes the row frameset.

</FRAMESET>                   ◄——   Closes the column frameset.

</HTML>
```

Script 6.2 This frameset has two frames that each occupy half of the browser window.

```
File  Edit  Search  Help

<HTML>
<HEAD><TITLE>A simple frameset</TITLE></HEAD>

<FRAMESET COLS="50%, 50%">
      <FRAME SRC="left.html">
      <FRAME SRC="right.html">
    </FRAMESET>
</FRAMESET>

</HTML>
```

Script 6.3 You can set the background color with an onload event. In referring to frames by number, don't forget to start counting at 0.

```
File  Edit  Search  Help

<HTML>
<HEAD><TITLE>A simple frameset</TITLE></HEAD>

<SCRIPT LANGUAGE="VBSCRIPT">
<!--
  Sub Window_onLoad
    Window.frames(0).document.bgColor =
"CCFF66"
    End Sub
-->
</SCRIPT>

<FRAMESET COLS="50%, 50%">
      <FRAME SRC="left.html">
      <FRAME SRC="right.html">
    </FRAMESET>
</FRAMESET>

</HTML>
```

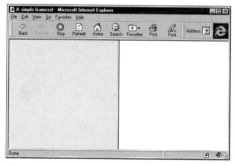

Figure 6.2 The background is now a beautiful lime green. The code changes the background color of the first frame—frame 0.

ACCESSING FRAMES BY NUMBER

Until now all of your scripts have been on the current page, so there's been no need to worry about where the script will execute. When you have frames on your page, however, you need to know how to access each frame individually.

The most basic way to access frames from VBScript is by number. The VBScript **Frame** object automatically creates a list of the frames on your page and you can access them by their number, or place, in the list. The first frame in the list is number 0, and it is referenced as

> window.frames(0)

You can simplify this reference as

> frames(0)

The second and third frames are **frames(1)** and **frames(2)** and so on.

To access frames by number:

1. Create a new blank HTML file and save it as **number.html**

2. Add the frameset shown in **Script 6.2.**

3. Create two blank HTML files and save them as **left.html** and **right.html**. These files will contain the content of two of the frames in your frameset.

4. Return to the **number.html** file and add the script shown in **Script 6.3** above the frameset.

5. Save the file and load it in your browser. The result should look like **Figure 6.2.**

ACCESSING A FRAME FROM ANOTHER FRAME

In the previous section, you changed the background color of a frame with this code:

```
Window.frames(0).document.bgColor =
"CCFF66"
```

This code works because it appears in the same file that created the frameset. Putting this code inside one of the frame files, like left.html, will cause an error. This is one of those programming gotchas, and it involves something called *scope*. The scope of an object describes where that object can be seen and used.

To access a frame from another frame, you need to add the Window object's **top** property, as shown in **Figure 6.3.**

```
Window.top.frames(0).document.bgColor =
"CCFF66"
```

Figure 6.3 The **top** property accesses the topmost window. In this example, the topmost window is the window that contains the frameset.

Script 6.4 Create a simple frameset.

```
File  Edit  Search  Help

<HTML>
<HEAD><TITLE>Accessing one frame from
another</TITLE></HEAD>

<FRAMESET COLS="100, *">
     <FRAME SRC="nav.html">
     <FRAME SRC="main.html">
   </FRAMESET>
</FRAMESET>

</HTML>
```

To change the color of the left frame from the right frame:

1. Create a new HTML file and save it as frames.html

2. Add the frameset shown in **Script 6.4** and save the file.

3. Create two blank HTML files and save them as nav.html and main.html

4. Load **Frames.html**. It should resemble **Figure 6.4.**

5. Add a script to nav.html, as shown in **Script 6.5.**

6. Save all of the files and reload frames.html. The result should resemble **Figure 6.5.**

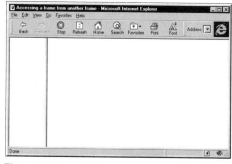

Figure 6.4 Script 6.4 loaded into Internet Explorer.

Script 6.5 Using the **top** property in **nav.html.**

```
File  Edit  Search  Help

<HTML>
<HEAD><TITLE>Navigation Bar</TITLE></HEAD>

<SCRIPT LANGUAGE="VBSCRIPT">
<!--
  Sub Window_onLoad
    Window.top.frames(1).document.bgColor =
"66FFCC"
  End Sub
-->
</SCRIPT>

<BODY>
</BODY>
</HTML>
```

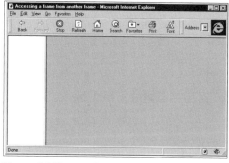

Figure 6.5 You can change the color of the righthand frame with code in the file for the lefthand frame.

ACCESSING FRAMES BY NAME

Accessing frames by their numbers becomes very complicated very quickly because you have to constantly pay attention to the internal numbering scheme of your scripts. Accessing frames by name is an alternative method that can be much easier. To do this, you name frames in HTML code and then access those names within VBScript. If number-based frames give you problems, this may be the answer.

In HTML, you name objects with the **NAME** attribute by simply placing the **NAME** attribute and an appropriate value in each **FRAME** tag, as shown in **Script 6.6.**

Easy, isn't it? Well, accessing these frames from VBScript is even easier. To change the background color of the right frame, you might write code like

> top.frames("LeftFrame").document.bgColor = "000000"

This code executes from any of the files that make up this frameset: the frameset itself, **left.html**, or right.html. All you have to do is substitute the name of the frame, in quotes, for the number you were using in earlier examples.

To access frames by name:

1. Create a new HTML file and save it as nameframe.html

2. Add a frameset to nameframe.html, as shown in **Script 6.7.**

3. Create two blank HTML files, and save them as top.html and bottom.html

Script 6.6 Referring to frames by name, rather than number, can make your frameset code easier to work with, especially as your site becomes more complex.

```
File  Edit  Search  Help

<HTML>
<HEAD><TITLE>Frames by Name</TITLE></HEAD>

<FRAMESET COLS="50%, 50%">
  <FRAME SRC="left.html" NAME="LeftFrame">
  <FRAME SRC="right.html" NAME="RightFrame">
</FRAMESET>

</HTML>
```

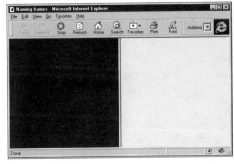

Figure 6.6 Color me black! Naming frames makes scripts easier to read.

Script 6.7 Remember, you must create the **top.html** and **bottom.html** files for this file to load properly.

```
File  Edit  Search  Help

<HTML>
<HEAD><TITLE>Frames by Name</TITLE></HEAD>

<FRAMESET ROWS="50%, 50%">
  <FRAME SRC="top.html" NAME="TopFrame">
  <FRAME SRC="bottom.html" NAME="BottomFrame">
</FRAMESET>

</HTML>
```

Script 6.8 The **top.html** file contains a group of command buttons.

```
File  Edit  Search  Help

<HTML>

<BODY BGCOLOR="#FFFFCC">
<FONT FACE="Arial" SIZE=5>
Enter a color value for the bottom frame</FONT>
<FORM>
    <INPUT TYPE=BUTTON NAME="btnWhite"
VALUE="White">
    <INPUT TYPE=BUTTON NAME="btnRed" VALUE="Red">
    <INPUT TYPE=BUTTON NAME="btnGreen"
VALUE="Green">
    <INPUT TYPE=BUTTON NAME="btnBlue"
VALUE="Blue">
</FORM>
</BODY>

</HTML>
```

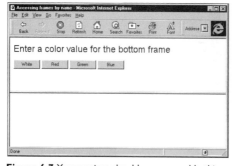

Figure 6.7 Your project should now resemble this—the final step is to add the scripting logic that makes it all come together.

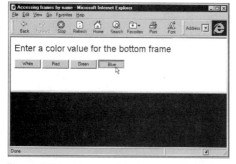

Figure 6.8 Clicking any of the buttons will change the background color of the bottom frame.

4. Edit **top.html** so it resembles **Script 6.8.**

5. Now add the script section shown in **Script 6.9** to **top.html,** above the body section.

6. Save all of the files and load **nameframe.html** in your browser. The result should resemble **Figure 6.8.**

Script 6.9 This script section creates events for each of the buttons. Remember, you can copy all this code from **http://www.internet-nexus.com/vbvqs**

```
File  Edit  Search  Help

<HTML>
<SCRIPT LANGUAGE="VBSCRIPT">
<!--
    Sub btnWhite_onClick
        Top.frames("BottomFrame").document.bgColor
= "white"
    End Sub

    Sub btnRed_onClick
        Top.frames("BottomFrame").document.bgColor
= "red"
    End Sub

    Sub btnGreen_onClick
        Top.frames("BottomFrame").document.bgColor
= "green"
    End Sub

    Sub btnBlue_onClick
        Top.frames("BottomFrame").document.bgColor
= "blue"
    End Sub
-->
</SCRIPT>

<BODY BGCOLOR="#FFFFCC">
<FONT FACE="Arial" SIZE=5>
Enter a color value for the bottom frame</FONT>
<FORM>
    <INPUT TYPE=BUTTON NAME="btnWhite"
VALUE="White">
    <INPUT TYPE=BUTTON NAME="btnRed" VALUE="Red">
    <INPUT TYPE=BUTTON NAME="btnGreen"
VALUE="Green">
    <INPUT TYPE=BUTTON NAME="btnBlue"
VALUE="Blue">
</FORM>
</BODY>

</HTML>
```

ACCESSING FRAMES BY NAME

TARGETING A FRAME

Navigational toolbars may be the most popular use of frames. Frames allow you to keep a toolbar in front of the user at all times, making the browsing experience more clear. To create a toolbar, you need to know how to target frames. When a user clicks a hyperlink in the navigational frame, you typically want to load the document in the content frame. Sometimes you will want to load a document into the full browser window as well.

In HTML, you target a frame by specifying the name of the frame with a **TARGET** attribute in the hyperlink, as shown in **Figure 6.9.** You can also use the top property to open the hyperlink in the full browser window, as shown in **Figure 6.10.**

With VBScript, it is easy to open new documents and, if you're using frames, to target specific frames. To open a new document, you simply use the **Location** object, which is accessed through the **location** property of the **Window** object.

To open a new document in the current frame:

1. Create an HTML file and save it as contain.html

2. Add a frameset with two columns as shown in **Script 6.10.**

Now you will have to create two files to fill the frameset.

```
<A HREF="http://www.microsoft.com"
TARGET="Content">Microsoft</A>
```

Figure 6.9 This code will open the link in the **Content** frame of your frameset, using the **TARGET** attribute.

```
<A HREF="http://www.microsoft.com"
TARGET="_top">Microsoft</A>
```

Figure 6.10 Targeting the top property will open the link in a new full browser window, leaving your frameset altogether.

Script 6.10 This HTML code creates a frameset with two columns.

```
File  Edit  Search  Help

<HTML>

<TITLE>Targeting the same frame</TITLE>

<FRAMESET COLS="150,*">
    <FRAME SRC="menu.html">
    <FRAME SRC="contents.html">
</FRAMESET>

</HTML>
```

Script 6.11 Menu.html is simple enough. It just sets the background color to yellow.

```
File  Edit  Search  Help
<HTML>

<BODY BGCOLOR="#FFFFCC">
</BODY>

</HTML>
```

Script 6.12 This file creates a form button that launches the Microsoft Web site in the current frame.

```
File  Edit  Search  Help
<HTML>

<BODY BGCOLOR="#CCFFFF">
<FORM>
  <INPUT TYPE="Button" VALUE="Microsoft"
   NAME="btnMicrosoft">
</FORM>
</BODY>

<SCRIPT LANGUAGE="VBSCRIPT">
<!--
  Sub btnMicrosoft_onClick
    location.href="http://www.microsoft.com"
  End Sub
-->
<SCRIPT>

</HTML>
```

3. Create the file shown in **Script 6.11** and save it as menu.html

4. Create another file, as shown in **Script 6.12**, and save it as contents.html

5. Make sure all of the files are saved and load contain.html into your Web browser. As shown in **Figure 6.11**, the Microsoft Web site is loaded in the same frame as the button.

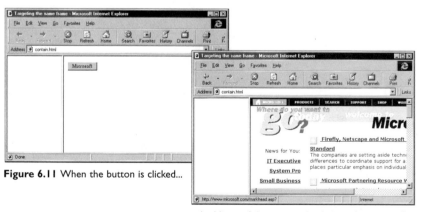

Figure 6.11 When the button is clicked...

...the Microsoft home page loads into the current frame.

CREATING A NAVIGATIONAL TOOLBAR

Creating a navigational toolbar requires that you understand how to target frames, so review the previous section if you haven't already.

In this example, the toolbar will be a list of text hyperlinks, but it could just as easily be a list of images (or a single imagemap) or a list of command buttons. The look and feel of your navigational toolbars is up to you.

The basic layout of the frameset will include a title frame at the top, and two lower frames: the leftmost frame will contain the navigational toolbar, and the rightmost frame will contain the content. You load pages into the content frame by clicking one of the buttons in the navigational toolbar.

To create a navigational toolbar with frames:

1. Create a new HTML file and save it as target.html

2. Add the script section shown in **Script 6.13.**

3. Create the HTML file and save it as title.html. This file will fill the title frame.

4. Add the script section shown in **Script 6.14.**

5. Now, create an HTML file as shown in **Script 6.15** and save it as content.html

(Continued on the next page.)

Script 6.15 Content.html will hold the content.

```
File  Edit  Search  Help

<HTML>

<HEAD>
<TITLE>Content</HTML>
</HEAD>

<BODY BG COLOR="#FFFFFF">
</BODY>
<HTML>
```

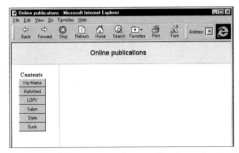

Figure 6.12 This is a simple example of a navigational toolbar with an open content frame.

Script 6.13 This piece of frameset code will create the layout shown in **Figure 6.12.**

```
File  Edit  Search  Help

<HTML>

<HEAD>
<TITLE>The target file</HTML>
</HEAD>

<FRAMESET ROWS="55, *" FRAMEBORDER=0>
  <FRAME SRC="title.html" NAME="Title">
  <FRAMESET COLS="125, *">
    <FRAME SRC="navtext.html" NAME="Nav">
    <FRAME SRC="content.html" NAME="Content">
  </FRAME>
</FRAMESET>

</HTML>
```

Script 6.14 This code creates the title.

```
File  Edit  Search  Help

<HTML>

<HEAD>
<TITLE>Title</HTML>
</HEAD>

<BODY BGCOLOR="#FFCC66">

<CENTER><FONT FACE="Arial" SIZE=4>
Online publications</FONT></CENTER>

</BODY>

</HTML>
```

Script 6.16 For the buttons to have any effect, you'll need to add VBScript **onClick** event handlers for each button so that they load the proper Web sites into the contents frame when clicked.

```
File   Edit   Search   Help

<HTML>

<HEAD>
<TITLE>The navigational text</HTML>
</HEAD>

<SCRIPT LANGUAGE="VBSCRIPT">
<!--
   Sub btnHipMama_onClick

Top.frames("Content").location.href="http://www.
hipmama.com"
   End Sub

   Sub btnHotWired_onClick

Top.frames("Content").location.href="http://www.
hotwired.com"
   End Sub

   Sub btnLOFY_onClick

Top.frames("Content").location.href="http://www.
lofy.com"
   End Sub

   Sub btnSalon_onClick

Top.frames("Content").location.href="http://www.
salon.com"
   End Sub

   Sub btnSlate_onClick

Top.frames("Content").location.href="http://www.
slate.com"
   End Sub

   Sub btnSuck_onClick

Top.frames("Content").location.href="http://www.
suck.com"
   End Sub

-->
</SCRIPT>

<BODY BGCOLOR="#FFFFCC">
<CENTER>
<FORM><B>Contents</B>
<BR><INPUT TYPE=BUTTON NAME="btnHipMama"
VALUE="Hip Mama">
```

(Continued from the previous page.)

6. Most of the action occurs in the navtext.html file. Create that file now using **Script 6.16** as a guide.

7. Add the code shown in **Script 6.17** above the body section in navtext.html

8. Save all your files and check it out!

Script 6.17 This code creates a form with six command buttons that form your navigational toolbar. Remember, you can copy all this code from **http://www.internet-nexus.com/vbvqs**

```
File   Edit   Search   Help

<HTML>

<HEAD>
<TITLE>The navigational text</HTML>
</HEAD>

<BODY BGCOLOR="#FFFFCC">
<CENTER>
<FORM><B>Contents</B>
<BR><INPUT TYPE=BUTTON NAME="btnHipMama"
VALUE="Hip Mama">
<BR><INPUT TYPE=BUTTON NAME="btnHotWired"
VALUE="HotWired">
<BR><INPUT TYPE=BUTTON NAME="btnLOFY"
VALUE="LOFY">
<BR><INPUT TYPE=BUTTON NAME="btnSalon"
VALUE="Salon">
<BR><INPUT TYPE=BUTTON NAME="btnSlate"
VALUE="Slate">
<BR><INPUT TYPE=BUTTON NAME="btnSuck"
VALUE="Suck">
</FORM>
</CENTER>
</BODY>

</HTML>
```

Working with Documents

The **Document** object controls the HTML document currently loaded in the browser. Like the **Window** object, the **Document** object contains other objects. These contained objects include such things as hyperlinks, forms, buttons, and ActiveX controls. To use any of the **Document** object properties and methods, you simply have to use the word **Document** followed by a property or method name in your script. The **write** method is used like this:

```
Document.write("Hello, world")
```

The **Document** object has a number of properties and methods. In this chapter, you will explore some of the things you can do with these tools.

DOCUMENT OBJECT PROPERTIES AND METHODS

The Document object introduces the properties shown in **Table 7.1.** A quick look through the list of properties reveals some pretty familiar faces. Most of these properties are script-based ways to alter Web page attributes that can also be accomplished with pure HTML. Why use VBScript, then, to set the background color of the page or determine the color of text? For one thing, you can set many of these attributes at any time with VBScript. Using pure HTML, you can only set them once, as the page loads. You might want to change these attributes in response to a user request, or after a specific period of time has elapsed.

One of the best reasons to use VBScript to alter these properties is that it allows you to provide a unique experience for Internet Explorer users. You could set these attributes differently in HTML and VBScript and ensure that IE users experience a different look and feel when they visit your site.

The Document object introduces the methods shown in **Table 7.2.** The Document object methods are divided into two types: those that write text directly to the document (write and writeLn) and those that deal with something called a document stream (clear, close, and open).

Table 7.1 The properties of the **Document** object.

PROPERTY	WHAT IT IS
aLinkColor	contains the active link color for the document
anchors	refers to the Anchor object contained by the Document object
bgColor	contains the document's background color
cookie	contains the cookie for the document
fgColor	contains the document's foreground (text) color
forms	refers to the Form object contained by the Document object
lastModified	contains the date the document was last modified
linkColor	contains the link color for the document
links	refers to the Link object contained by the Document object
location	contains the URL information for the document
referrer	contains the URL of the document the user visited before the current document
title	contains the title of the document
vLinkColor	contains the visited link color for the document

Table 7.2 The methods of the **Document** object.

METHOD	WHAT IT IS
clear	clears a document stream and writes any output to the screen
close	closes a document stream and writes any output to the screen
open	opens a document stream so that subsequent writes occur simultaneously
write	writes a string to the document
writeLn	writes a string and a new line character to the document

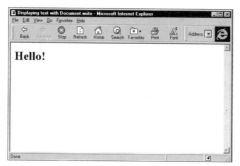

Figure 7.1 Text displayed with **Document.write** will use the current HTML style.

Script 7.1 Here are two examples where the **write** object will use the formatting in place when it appears. The first mention will appear as Arial, with a maroon color, the second as Times New Roman in black.

```
File  Edit  Search  Help

<HTML>
<HEAD><TITLE>Displaying text</TITLE></HEAD>

<BODY BGCOLOR="#FFFFFF">

<FONT FACE="Arial" SIZE=5 COLOR="Maroon">
<SCRIPT LANGUAGE="VBSCRIPT">
<!--
   Document.write("Welcome to my VBScript home-
page")
-->
</SCRIPT>
</FONT>
<P>
<FONT FACE="Times New Roman" SIZE=3
COLOR="Black">

<SCRIPT>
<!--
   Document.write("The write method of the Docu-
ment object will pick up the current HTML style
and use it to display the text you specify.")
-->
</SCRIPT LANGUAGE="VBSCRIPT">
</FONT>

</BODY>
</HTML>
```

DISPLAYING TEXT

VBScript's most frequently used method is **write**. The **write** method belongs to the **Document** object and allows you to write text to the screen. The text you display with the **write** method is placed directly into the document at the point the script appears, so it picks up whatever HTML styles are described in your document. For example, the following code will display the word Hello! using the <H1> (Heading one) style:

```
<H1>
<SCRIPT LANGUAGE="VBSCRIPT">
<!--
   Document.write("Hello!")
-->
</SCRIPT>
</H1>
```

To display text:

1. Create a new, blank HTML file and save it as **text.html**

2. Add the code in **Script 7.1** inside the body section.

3. Save the file and view it in your browser. The result should resemble **Figure 7.2**.

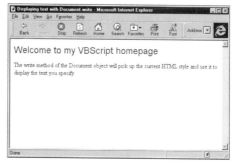

Figure 7.2 The **write** method picks up the current HTML style and runs with it.

DISPLAYING HTML

The **write** method also allows you to specify any HTML tag you wish within the text. Basically, anything you can display with HTML, you can display with VBScript.

One important thing to note is that the **write** method uses double quotes to surround the text it displays. Because of this, you must change any double quotes in HTML to single quotes, or suffer the embarrassment of an error message.

To display HTML text:

1. Create a new, blank HTML file and save it as display.html

2. Add the script section shown in **Script 7.2** inside the body section.

3. Save the file and load it in your browser. The result should resemble **Figure 7.4.**

Tips:

- One reason to use **write** instead of standard HTML tags is that **write** methods can be placed in procedures and functions. If you have text to display several times in the same page, it makes sense to place some **write** methods in a procedure and then call the procedure when you need to. That way, if you need to change the text, you are only changing it in one place, not searching through your HTML looking for each occurrence.

- The **write** method has an interesting—but limited—sibling called **writeLn**. The difference is that **writeLn** appends a new line character to the end of each string it outputs. The limitation is that your browser will not display a new line unless you place the **writeLn** between some **<PRE>** tags. Don't bother. Just use **write** instead.

Figure 7.3 You can specify HTML tags within the text you display with the **write** method.

Script 7.2 The **write** method can be used to display any HTML tag. This script section displays a variety of standard HTML.

```
File  Edit  Search  Help

<HTML>
<HEAD><TITLE>Displaying HTML text</TITLE></HEAD>
<BODY BGCOLOR="#FFFFFF">

<SCRIPT>
<!--
    Document.write("<FONT FACE='Arial' SIZE=5
COLOR='#336699'>")
    Document.write("Visual Basic Script
pages</FONT><BR>")
    Document.write("<FONT FACE='Times New Roman'
SIZE=4>")
    Document.write("<A HREF='http://
www.microsoft.com/vbscript'>")
    Document.write("Microsoft's VBScript
page</A><BR>")
    Document.write("<A HREF='http://www.internet-
nexus.com'>")
    Document.write("Internet Nexus</A>")
    Document.write("</FONT>")
-->
</SCRIPT>

</BODY>
</HTML>
```

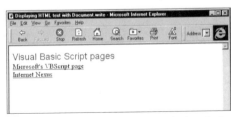

Figure 7.4 You can use the **write** method to display HTML that is meant only for Internet Explorer users if you like.

Table 7.3 <BODY> tag attributes and their VBScript alternatives.

ATTRIBUTE	VBSCRIPT	WHAT IT DOES
ALINK	AlinkColor	determines the color of an active hyperlink
BGCOLOR	BgColor	determines the background color of the document
LINK	LinkColor	determines the color of an unvisited hyperlink
TEXT	FgColor	determines the default color of text
VLINK	VlinkColor	determines the color of a visited hyperlink

Script 7.3 This HTML code sets the basic characteristics of the <BODY>.

```
File   Edit   Search   Help

<HTML>
<HEAD><TITLE>Magic 8 Ball</TITLE></HEAD>

<BODY BGCOLOR="Black" TEXT="Black" LINK="White"
VLINK="White" ALINK="White">

</HTML>
```

Script 7.4 The "MagicEightBall" you see in the **Document.write** method is a function call. Of course, you have to create that function for this to work.

```
File   Edit   Search   Help

<HTML>
<HEAD><TITLE>Magic 8 Ball</TITLE></HEAD>

<BODY BGCOLOR="Black" TEXT="Black" LINK="White"
VLINK="White" ALINK="White">

<P><CENTER><A HREF="" NAME="lnkVBS">Silently
make your wish and then move the mouse over
this text to get your answer</A>

<SCRIPT LANGUAGE="VBSCRIPT">
<!--
   Document.write("<BR><BR><BR><FONT SIZE=7>" &
MagicEightBall & "</FONT></CENTER>")

-->
</SCRIPT>

</HTML>
```

WORKING WITH DOCUMENT ATTRIBUTES

VBScript provides a slew of properties that mimic the behavior of <BODY> tag attributes. **Table 7.3** lists several of these attributes and their VBScript equivalents. When you specify these attributes using plain HTML, it might look something like

```
<BODY BGCOLOR="White" TEXT="Black"
LINK="Blue" VLINK="Blue" ALINK="Red">
```

In this particular case, the background of the HTML will be white, the text color is black, unvisited and visited links are blue, and active links are red. To achieve the same effect with VBScript, you could use the following code:

```
Sub Window_onLoad

   Document.bgColor = "White"

   Document.fgColor = "Black"

   Document.linkColor = "Blue"

   Document.vLinkColor = "Blue"

   Document.aLinkColor = "Red"

End Sub
```

OK, let's create a VBScript Magic Eight Ball!

To get and set document attributes:

1. Create a new, blank HTML file called **8ball.html** and set the <BODY> tag as shown in **Script 7.3**.

2. Now, add the code to the body section, as shown in **Script 7.4**.

(Continued on the next page.)

(Continued from the previous page.)

3. Add the MagicEightBall function and the script section that contains it above the body section, as shown in **Script 7.5.**

4. Finally, to tie the whole thing together, you need to handle the event that occurs when the user moves the mouse pointer over the hyperlink. This is done with a **mouseover** event placed in the script section with the MagicEightBall function, as shown in **Script 7.6.**

5. Now save the file and check it out! Your result should resemble **Figure 7.5.**

Tips:

■ There are two ways to specify colors with VBScript: by name (Document.bgColor = "White"), or by hex value (Document.bgColor = "FFFFFF"). Unlike plain HTML, you leave the pound sign off when using a hex value to specify a color.

■ Here's one good reason to set these attributes with VBScript: they can be changed at will. With plain HTML, you can only control the document attributes once, when the page loads.

Figure 7.5 The Magic Eight Ball functions just like the real thing!

Script 7.5 Add the words of wisdom to your Magic Eight Ball.

```
File  Edit  Search  Help

<HTML>
<HEAD><TITLE>Magic 8 Ball</TITLE></HEAD>

<SCRIPT LANGUAGE="VBSCRIPT">
<!--
   Function MagicEightBall()
     Dim WordsOfWisdom(7), Num
     Randomize
     WordsOfWisdom(0) = "Yes, definitely"
     WordsOfWisdom(1) = "Maybe"
     WordsOfWisdom(2) = "Try again later"
     WordsOfWisdom(3) = "Maybe not"
     WordsOfWisdom(4) = "Probably"
     WordsOfWisdom(5) = "I am sure of it"
     WordsOfWisdom(6) = "You bet"
     num = Int(Rnd() * ((7 - 1) + 1))
     MagicEightBall = WordsOfWisdom(Num) & _
                      "<BR><BR><BR><FONT
SIZE=2>" & _
                      "Press REFRESH to make
another wish</FONT>"
   End Function
-->
</SCRIPT>

<BODY BGCOLOR="Black" TEXT="Black" LINK="White"
VLINK="White" ALINK="White">
```

Script 7.6 This **onMouseOver** event ties the whole thing together, creating responses as the user's mouse pointer passes over the screen.

```
File  Edit  Search  Help

<HTML>
<HEAD><TITLE>Magic 8 Ball</TITLE></HEAD>

<SCRIPT LANGUAGE="VBSCRIPT">
<!--
   Sub lnkVBS_onMouseOver
     Document.fgColor = "White"
     Document.linkColor = "Black"
     Document.vLinkColor = "Black"
     Document.aLinkColor = "Black"
   End Sub

   Function MagicEightBall()
     Dim WordsOfWisdom(7), Num
     Randomize
     WordsOfWisdom(0) = "Yes, definitely"
     WordsOfWisdom(1) = "Maybe"
     WordsOfWisdom(2) = "Try again later"
     WordsOfWisdom(3) = "Maybe not"
     WordsOfWisdom(4) = "Probably"
```

Last modified on Sun Mar 23 13:21:18 1997

Figure 7.6 The default display of **lastModified** is a mess.

Script 7.7 Separate the first seven characters of the **lastModified** property, which contain the day and the month. From that string, separate the month, which is the last three letters, off the end.

```
File  Edit  Search  Help

<HTML>
<HEAD><TITLE>Date last modified</TITLE></HEAD>

<BODY BGCOLOR="#FFFFFF">

<SCRIPT LANGUAGE="VBSCRIPT">
<!--
  Document.write("This page was last modified
on ")
' First, get the month
  MyMonth = Left(Document.lastModified, 7)
  MyMonth = Right(MyMonth, 3)

-->
</SCRIPT>
</BODY>
</HTML>
```

Script 7.8 The **Case** statements convert the months to numbers, the first part of our date string.

```
File  Edit  Search  Help

  Document.write("This page was last modified
on ")
' First, get the month
  MyMonth = Left(Document.lastModified, 7)
  MyMonth = Right(MyMonth, 3)

  Select Case MyMonth
      Case "Jan" MyDate = "1/"
      Case "Feb" MyDate = "2/"
      Case "Mar" MyDate = "3/"
      Case "Apr" MyDate = "4/"
      Case "May" MyDate = "5/"
      Case "Jun" MyDate = "6/"
      Case "Jul" MyDate = "7/"
      Case "Aug" MyDate = "8/"
      Case "Sep" MyDate = "9/"
      Case "Oct" MyDate = "10/"
      Case "Nov" MyDate = "11/"
      Case Else MyDate = "12/"
  End Select

-->
</SCRIPT>
</BODY>
</HTML>
```

SHOWING THE LAST DATE MODIFIED

Many Web sites display the date that each page was last modified. VBScript provides a way for you to automate this procedure. The **Document** object's lastModified property contains the date and time a page was last modified. Unfortunately, the default output is a little raw, as shown in **Figure 7.6.**

Fortunately, you can strip off parts of the output to construct a nicer looking string using the proper string and date functions.

The **Date** function produces the "date format," where forward slashes separate the number of the month, day, and year:

> 3/23/97

The goal is to get the display from lastModified into a **date** format. Once you have the output in this format, you can further edit it to your liking.

This is a long but very useful script that's not all that difficult and is something you might want to use over and over. To save time, you can copy the code from the Web site for this book:

> http://www.internet-nexus.com/vbvqs

To display the last modified date:

1. Create a new, blank HTML file and save it as lastmod.html

2. Start a new script section within the body, with the code in **Script 7.7,** to separate the day and the month.

3. Add a series of **Case** statements right after the code from the previous step, as shown in **Script 7.8.**

(Continued on the next page.)

(Continued from the previous page.)

4. Separate the day and the year out of the lastModified string and add them to the date string below the case statements, as shown in **Script 7.9.** You now have a date that conforms to the "date format."

5. **Script 7.10** converts the month of our date into an English month name.

6. All that's left to do now is to display the date with the **write** method. Add code as shown in **Script 7.11.**

7. Save the file and view it in your browser. The result should resemble **Figure 7.7.**

Script 7.11 The output will be the month name, a space, the day of our modified date, a comma, a space, and then the year portion of **lastModified.**

```
File  Edit  Search  Help

     Case 11 MyMonthName =   "November"
     Case Else MyMonthName =  "December"
  End Select

Document.write(MyMonthName & " " & Day(MyDate)
& ", " & Right(Document.lastModified, 4))

-->
</SCRIPT>
</BODY>
</HTML>
```

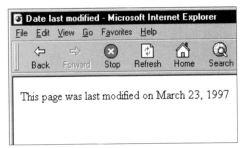

```
Date last modified - Microsoft Internet Explorer
File  Edit  View  Go  Favorites  Help

  Back   Forward   Stop   Refresh   Home   Search


  This page was last modified on March 23, 1997
```

Figure 7.7 Now that's a nice looking date! The code is long, but very handy. You can use it again and again throughout your sites.

Script 7.9 The ninth and tenth characters of the whole string represent the day. This code adds it to the date string. The code also adds a two-character version of the year to our date string.

```
File  Edit  Search  Help

        Case "Oct" MyDate = "10/"
        Case "Nov" MyDate = "11/"
        Case Else MyDate = "12/"
     End Select

  'Next, get the day
  MyDay = Left(Document.lastModified, 10)
  MyDay = Right(MyDay, 2)

  MyDate = MyDate & MyDay & "/"

  'Now, the year
  MyYear = Right(Document.lastModified, 2)
  MyDate = MyDate & MyYear

  -->
</SCRIPT>
```

Script 7.10 Add the English month name.

```
File  Edit  Search  Help

  'Next, get the day
  MyDay = Left(Document.lastModified, 10)
  MyDay = Right(MyDay, 2)

  MyDate = MyDate & MyDay & "/"

  'Now, the year
  MyYear = Right(Document.lastModified, 2)
  MyDate = MyDate & MyYear

  Select Case Month(MyDate)
     Case 1 MyMonthName = "January"
     Case 2 MyMonthName = "February"
     Case 3 MyMonthName = "March"
     Case 4 MyMonthName = "April"
     Case 5 MyMonthName = "May"
     Case 6 MyMonthName = "June"
     Case 7 MyMonthName = "July"
     Case 8 MyMonthName = "August"
     Case 9 MyMonthName = "September"
     Case 10 MyMonthName =  "October"
     Case 11 MyMonthName =  "November"
     Case Else MyMonthName =  "December"
  End Select

  -->
</SCRIPT>
</BODY>
</HTML>
```

Script 7.12 Here's the entire script to display the date in a more readable format. The script is long, but fairly simple.

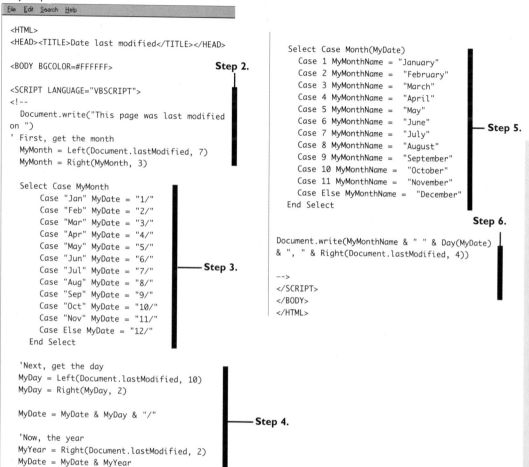

```
File  Edit  Search  Help

<HTML>
<HEAD><TITLE>Date last modified</TITLE></HEAD>

<BODY BGCOLOR=#FFFFFF>                           Step 2.

<SCRIPT LANGUAGE="VBSCRIPT">
<!--
   Document.write("This page was last modified
on ")
' First, get the month
   MyMonth = Left(Document.lastModified, 7)
   MyMonth = Right(MyMonth, 3)

   Select Case MyMonth
        Case "Jan" MyDate = "1/"
        Case "Feb" MyDate = "2/"
        Case "Mar" MyDate = "3/"
        Case "Apr" MyDate = "4/"
        Case "May" MyDate = "5/"
        Case "Jun" MyDate = "6/"
        Case "Jul" MyDate = "7/"            Step 3.
        Case "Aug" MyDate = "8/"
        Case "Sep" MyDate = "9/"
        Case "Oct" MyDate = "10/"
        Case "Nov" MyDate = "11/"
        Case Else MyDate = "12/"
   End Select

   'Next, get the day
   MyDay = Left(Document.lastModified, 10)
   MyDay = Right(MyDay, 2)

   MyDate = MyDate & MyDay & "/"            Step 4.

   'Now, the year
   MyYear = Right(Document.lastModified, 2)
   MyDate = MyDate & MyYear


   Select Case Month(MyDate)
        Case 1 MyMonthName =  "January"
        Case 2 MyMonthName =  "February"
        Case 3 MyMonthName =  "March"
        Case 4 MyMonthName =  "April"
        Case 5 MyMonthName =  "May"
        Case 6 MyMonthName =  "June"       Step 5.
        Case 7 MyMonthName =  "July"
        Case 8 MyMonthName =  "August"
        Case 9 MyMonthName =  "September"
        Case 10 MyMonthName =  "October"
        Case 11 MyMonthName =  "November"
        Case Else MyMonthName =  "December"
   End Select
                                            Step 6.
Document.write(MyMonthName & " " & Day(MyDate)
& ", " & Right(Document.lastModified, 4))

-->
</SCRIPT>
</BODY>
</HTML>
```

DISPLAYING THE CURRENT DOCUMENT LOCATION

The **Document** object's **location** property contains the document's URL or location on your local computer, as shown in **Figure 7.8.** The basic form looks like

Document.write("<P>The URL of this page is " & Document.location)

This property is useful if you have a frame-based page and the user wants to display a particular document in the full height and width of the browser. The following steps show you how to do this.

To display the location of the current document:

1. Create a new, blank HTML file called locationframe. Then, create the frameset shown in **Script 7.13.**

2. Create a file called title.html. This can be blank, or you can add some sort of title if you like.

3. Finally, create a file with the main frame in it as shown in **Script 7.14.** Save the file as locationmain.html

4. Now save the file and view it in your browser. The result should resemble **Figure 7.9.**

Figure 7.9 When you click the hyperlink, the document in the lower frame displays itself in the full browser window and the hyperlink disappears!

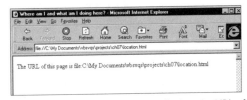

Figure 7.8 The **location** property displays the URL of the current document.

Script 7.13 A frames-based page requires you to create three files: one containing the frameset and two normal HTML pages. This file contains the frameset.

```
File  Edit  Search  Help

<HTML>
<HEAD><TITLE>The location
property</TITLE></HEAD>

<FRAMESET ROWS="50, *" FRAMEBORDER=0>
    <FRAME NAME="title" SRC="title.html">
    <FRAME NAME="main" SRC="locationmain.html">
<FRAMESET>

</HTML>
```

Script 7.14 The file **locationmain.html** contains the scripting that allows the user to view the document in the full height and width of the browser.

```
File  Edit  Search  Help

<HTML>
<HEAD><TITLE>The main frame</TITLE></HEAD>

<BODY BGCOLOR="#FFFFFF">

<SCRIPT LANGUAGE="VBSCRIPT">
<!--
    If Top.frames.count = 2 Then
        Document.write("<CENTER>")
        Document.write("Click <A HREF='")
        Document.write(Document.location & "'
TARGET='_top'>")
        Document.write("HERE</A> to view in full
browser")
        Document.write("</CENTER>")
    End If
    Document.write("<BR><BR>The text of the
document goes here")
-->
</SCRIPT>
</BODY>
</HTML>
```

Script 7.15 Add form buttons to **history.html.**

```
File  Edit  Search  Help

<HTML>
<HEAD><TITLE>Going back and
forward</TITLE></HEAD>

<BODY BGCOLOR="#FFFFFF">

<FORM>
  <INPUT NAME="btnBack" VALUE="Go back"
TYPE=BUTTON>
  <INPUT NAME="btnForward" VALUE="Go forward"
TYPE=BUTTON>

</BODY>
</HTML>
```

Script 7.16 The event handlers in this script section respond to the user clicking the command buttons.

```
File  Edit  Search  Help

<HTML>
<HEAD><TITLE>Going back and
forward</TITLE></HEAD>

<SCRIPT LANGUAGE="VBSCRIPT">
<!--
  Sub btnBack_onClick
    Top.history.back
  End Sub

  Sub btnForward_onClick
    Top.history.forward
  End Sub
-->
</SCRIPT>

<BODY BGCOLOR="#FFFFFF">

<FORM>
  <INPUT NAME="btnBack" VALUE="Go back"
TYPE=BUTTON>
  <INPUT NAME="btnForward" VALUE="Go forward"
TYPE=BUTTON>

</BODY>
</HTML>
```

CREATING BACK AND FORWARD BUTTONS

VBScript's **History** object has **back** and **forward** methods that mimic the user clicking the Back and Forward buttons on the browser. The basic form of each looks like

history.back n

history.forward n

Using the n parameter, you can determine how many pages backward or forward the browser will jump, just as if the user had clicked the navigation buttons in the browser.

To create your own back and forward buttons:

1. Create a new HTML file and save it as history.html

2. Add the form and command buttons to the body section, as shown in **Script 7.15.**

3. Now, add the scripting section shown in **Script 7.16** above the body to add event handlers for each of the button's **onClick** events.

4. Save the file and check it out in your browser. The result should resemble **Figure 7.10.**

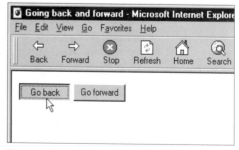

Figure 7.10 The command buttons mimic the behavior of the browser window's Back and Forward buttons.

GETTING THE CURRENT DOCUMENT TITLE

The **Document** object has a **title** property that allows you to get the title of the current document. **Title** is a read-only property, so you won't be able to change the document's title, just copy it. You can set the title of a document with the HTML **<TITLE>** tag, which has to be located in the HEAD section like:

    <HEAD>

    <TITLE>Document title</TITLE>

    </HEAD>

You can later display the title with the following script:

    Document.write(Document.title)

In the following steps, you create a script section that outputs the title of the current document in "Heading 1" style.

To get the title of the current document:

1. Create a new HTML file, as shown in **Script 7.17,** and save it as **titlename.html**

2. Now, add the script section shown in **Script 7.18** to the body section.

3. Save the file and view it in your browser. The result should resemble **Figure 7.11.**

Script 7.17 The humble beginnings of **titlename.html.**

```
File  Edit  Search  Help

<HTML>
<HEAD><TITLE>Welcome to my VBScript home
page!</TITLE></HEAD>

<BODY BGCOLOR="#FFFFFF">

</BODY>
</HTML>
```

Script 7.18 This script section will display the title of the document with a Heading 1 style.

```
File  Edit  Search  Help

<HTML>
<HEAD><TITLE>Welcome to my VBScript home
page!</TITLE></HEAD>

<SCRIPT LANGUAGE="VBSCRIPT">
<!--
   Document.write("<H1>" & Document.title &
"</H1>")
-->
</SCRIPT>

<BODY BGCOLOR="#FFFFFF">

</BODY>
</HTML>
```

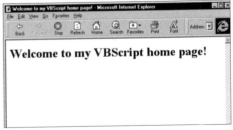

Figure 7.11 Here's one way to ensure that your title text and document title are identical.

GETTING THE CURRENT DOCUMENT TITLE

Script 7.19 This script section will display the title of the document with a Heading 1 style.

```
File   Edit   Search   Help

HTML>
<HEAD><TITLE>Using the href
property</TITLE></HEAD>

<BODY BGCOLOR="#FFFFFF">
<FORM><CENTER>
  <INPUT TYPE=BUTTON NAME="btnBigTent"
VALUE="Big Tent">
  <INPUT TYPE=BUTTON NAME="btnHipMama"
VALUE="Hip Mama">
  <INPUT TYPE=BUTTON NAME="btnLOFY"
VALUE="LOFY">
  <INPUT TYPE=BUTTON NAME="btnNexus"
VALUE="Internet Nexus">
  </CENTER>
</FORM>
</BODY>
</HTML>
```

Script 7.20 This script uses the **href** property to load a new document into the browser window.

```
File   Edit   Search   Help

HTML>
<HEAD><TITLE>Using the href
property</TITLE></HEAD>

<BODY BGCOLOR="#FFFFFF">

<SCRIPT LANGUAGE="VBSCRIPT">
<!--
  Sub btnBigTent_onClick
    Top.location.href =
"http://www.bigtent.com"
  End Sub

  Sub btnHipMama_onClick
    Top.location.href =
"http://www.hipmama.com"
  End Sub

  Sub btnLOFY_onClick
    Top.location.href = "http://www.lofy.com"
  End Sub

  Sub btnNexus_onClick
    Top.location.href = "http://www.internet-
nexus.com"
  End Sub
-->
</SCRIPT>

<BODY BGCOLOR="#FFFFFF">
```

Creating a Navigational Toolbar

Chapter 6 shows how to create a navigational toolbar with frames. You also do this by using the **Location** object's **href** property to load a new document. The **Location** object is typically accessed through the location property of the **Window** object like

MyURL = Window.location.href

If you set the **href** property to a new address, the window that contains the **Location** object will jump to the new location.

To load a new document:

1. Create a new, blank HTML file with a white background and save it as href.html

2. Add the code shown in **Script 7.19** to add four command buttons.

3. Now, create a VBScript to handle the onClick event for each of these buttons, as shown in **Script 7.20**.

4. Save the file and view it in your browser. The result should resemble **Figure 7.12**.

Figure 7.12 Using the built-in form buttons and the location object, you can easily create a professional looking navigational toolbar.

USING THE ANCHORS PROPERTY

In creating long HTML documents, it's often customary to add HTML bookmarks—sometimes called *anchors*—that let the user jump from location to location throughout the page. You can automate this functionality with VBScript by using the **anchors** property of the **Document** object.

The **anchors** property contains a list of all of the anchors that exist in a document. Like other list properties, anchors is an array that counts from 0, and looks like

Document.anchors(x)

The x represents the anchor to which you are referring, such as **Document.anchors(1)**, **Document.anchors(2)**, and so on.

The anchors property can find out the number of anchors in the current document with the *length* property:

Num = Document.anchors.length

To create a list of anchors at the bottom of a page:

1. Create a new, blank HTML file with a white background and save it as anchor.html

2. Add the code shown in **Script 7.21** to find the number of anchors.

3. Add the code shown in **Script 7.22** to loop through the anchors.

Note:

- This script must appear after the anchors appear: it will only display at the bottom of the page. The next section shows how to place these anchors in a frame, which can be a more useful navigational device.

Script 7.21 This code finds the number of anchors.

```
File  Edit  Search  Help

HTML>
<HEAD><TITLE>Using the href
property</TITLE></HEAD>

<BODY BGCOLOR="#FFFFFF">
<SCRIPT LANGUAGE="VBSCRIPT">
<!--
    Num = Document.anchors.length
-->
</SCRIPT>
</BODY>
</HTML>
```

Script 7.22 Now, add some anchors and the code to loop through them.

```
File  Edit  Search  Help

<HTML>
<HEAD><TITLE>Using the anchors
property</TITLE></HEAD>

<BODY BGCOLOR="#FFFFFF">

<A HREF="http://www.bigtent.com" NAME="big-
tent">Big Tent</A>
<BR><A HREF="http://www.hipmama.com" NAME="hip-
mama">Hip Mama</A>
<BR><A HREF="http://www.internet-nexus.com"
NAME="nexus">Internet Nexus</A>
<BR><A HREF="http://www.lofy.com"
NAME="lofy">LOFY</A>

<P>
<SCRIPT LANGUAGE="VBSCRIPT">
<!--
    Num = Document.anchors.length

    Document.write "The anchors on this " & _
       "page has the following names:"

    For x = 0 to Num - 1
       Document.write "<BR>" & _
          Document.anchors(x).name
    Next
-->
</SCRIPT>

</BODY>
</HTML>
```

Script 7.23 Dynamic HTML 'R' Us!

```
File  Edit  Search  Help

<HTML>
<HEAD><TITLE>Creating a new document with
VBScript</TITLE></HEAD>

<SCRIPT LANGUAGE="VBSCRIPT">
<!--
  Sub Button1_onClick
    Document.open "text.html"
    Document.write "<H1>Welcome to the new
document</H1>"
    Document.close
  End Sub
-->
</SCRIPT>

<BODY>

<FORM>Click the button to load a new document
  <BR><INPUT TYPE=BUTTON NAME="Button1"
VALUE="Make it so">
</FORM>

</BODY>
```

Figure 7.13 Click the button and—
voila!—a new document is created.

Script 7.24 This frameset contains two frames that run from top to bottom. The left frame is 125 pixels wide and the right frame takes up the remainder of the browser window.

```
File  Edit  Search  Help

<HTML>
<HEAD><TITLE>Anchor Frameset</TITLE></HEAD>

<FRAMESET COLS="125, *">
  <FRAME NAME="contents" SRC="contents.html">
  <FRAME NAME="main" SRC="anchor.html">
<FRAMESET>
<BODY></BODY>

</HTML>
```

USING OPEN AND CLOSE METHODS

The **open** and **close** methods are used to wipe out an existing document and write a new one. Consider the code shown in **Script 7.23.** This code uses the open and close methods to erase the existing document and display a new one. When the button is clicked, **Document.open** is called. Then, a new heading is displayed and the new document is closed. It's as if the original document—the one with the command button—never existed.

The **open** and **close** methods allow you to create the dynamic table of content frame suggested in the last section.

To create a document table of contents:

1. This example uses three files: a frameset and two normal HTML files. Create a file as shown in **Script 7.24** and save it as anchorframe.html

2. Now, create contents.html as shown in **Script 7.25.** This is a simple file since we are going to erase it and rewrite it later with VBScript.

(Continued on the next page.)

Script 7.25 Yes, it's almost empty, but we're going to rewrite this with VBScript.

```
File  Edit  Search  Help

<HTML>
<HEAD><TITLE>Contents</TITLE></HEAD>

<BODY>
</BODY>
</HTML>
```

83

(Continued from the previous page.)

3. Create a new HTML file that resembles **Script 7.26.** Add some text between each of the bookmarks in your version. The bookmarks won't work properly if you don't separate them somewhat. Save the file as anchor.html

4. To create a table of contents in the first, empty frame, add a script before the body section as shown in **Script 7.27.**

5. Finally, you need to call the subroutine so that your table of contents is actually displayed. Add the code to anchor.html as shown in **Script 7.27.**

6. Now, save all the files and load them into your browser. The result should resemble **Figure 7.14.**

Note:

- If the frames references confuse you, please refer back to Chapter 6 for a refresher.

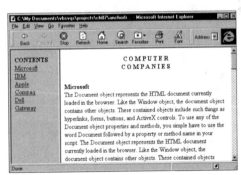

Figure 7.14 The table of contents in the left frame is automatically generated by scripting in the right frame. Pretty cool!

Script 7.26 Fill in the areas marked "add more text here" with something appropriate. Remember, you can find this code on this book's website **http://www.internet-nexus.com/vbvqs**

```
File  Edit  Search  Help

<HTML>
<HEAD><TITLE>Computer Companies</TITLE></HEAD>

<BODY BGCOLOR="#FFFFFF">

<CENTER><B>C O M P U T E R<BR>C O M P A N I E S
<BR><BR></B></CENTER>

<BR><A NAME="MS">
<B>Microsoft</B>
<BR> <!- add more text here ->

<P><A NAME="IBM">
<B>IBM</B>
<BR> <!- add more text here ->

<P><A NAME="Apple">
<B>Apple Computer</B>
<BR> <!- add more text here ->

<P><A NAME="Compaq">
<B>Compaq</B>
<BR> <!- add more text here ->

<P><A NAME="Dell">
<B>Dell</B>
<BR> <!- add more text here ->

<P><A NAME="GW2K">
<B>Gateway 2000</B>
<BR> <!- add more text here ->

</BODY>
</HTML>
```

Script 7.27 This script opens the first frame and displays a contents heading instead. The script loops through all of the anchors in the second frame's document and prints out the code necessary to make each anchor a hyperlink. When the list is completed, the new document is closed.

```
File   Edit   Search   Help

<HTML>

<HEAD><TITLE>Contents</TITLE></HEAD>

<SCRIPT LANGUAGE="VBSCRIPT">
<!--
   Sub MakeTOC
      Top.frames(0).document.open "text.html"
      Top.frames(0).document.write("<B>CONTENTS</B>")
      For x = 0 to
Top.frames(1).document.anchors.length - 1
         Top.frames(0).document.write("<BR>")
         Top.frames(0).document.write("<A     .
HREF='anchor.html#")
         Top.frames(0).document.write(Top.frames(1).
document.anchors(x).name)
         Top.frames(0).document.write("'
TARGET='main'>")
         Top.frames(0).document.write(Top.frames(1).
document.anchors(x).name)
         Top.frames(0).document.write("</A>")
      Next
      Top.frames(0).document.close
   End Sub
-->
</SCRIPT>

<BODY>

<SCRIPT LANGUAGE="VBSCRIPT">
<!--
   MakeTOC
-->
</SCRIPT>

</BODY>
</HTML>
```

Step 4 The script loops through all of the anchors in the second frame's document and prints out the code necessary to make each anchor a hyperlink. When the list is completed, the new document is closed.

Step 5 This script actually displays your table of contents.

USING OPEN AND CLOSE METHODS

USING FORMS

This chapter describes the lowest level of objects in the Internet Explorer Scripting Object Model: the **Form** and **Element** objects. These objects represent HTML forms and the user interface gadgets (like command buttons and text areas) that are contained in forms. The **Form** object is contained directly by the **Document** object. It in turn contains **Element** objects. One of VBScript's nicest features is its ability to control forms and form elements.

Before VBScript, validating forms required CGI scripts running on the Web server. Now, you can make sure that the user's input makes sense before sending it along to the server for processing. You can even validate input as the user moves from field to field (or element to element) within the form. No one likes to fill out forms, but VBScript makes it as painless as possible.

FORM OBJECT METHODS AND EVENTS

You can create forms with the HTML <FORM> tag. Each form can contain numerous elements, like command buttons, radio buttons, text areas, and more. Similarly, the forms object in VBScript contains the elements object.

Typically, you will access **Form** objects with the **forms** property of the **Document** object. The **forms** property is a list of the forms in the current document. The first form in a document can be accessed as:

    Document.forms(0)

You might also want to name your forms, which makes access easier. Consider the script shown in **Script 8.1,** which introduces a form named **Form1**. To access **Form1**, you would simply use the following code:

    Document.Form1

The **Form** object introduces one method and one event. Both are concerned with submitting a form. In HTML, a form is submitted when the user clicks a command button in the form, typically labeled "submit," that sends the information in the form to an application, generally a CGI application, on the server for processing.

The **Form** object introduces a single method, submit, as shown in **Table 8.1.** The submit method provides a way for you to submit the form. Normally, this is done by the user clicking a Submit button (a button whose TYPE is SUBMIT).

The **Form** object introduces the single event shown in **Table 8.2.** The onSubmit event occurs when the user presses the Submit button or when the submission is expedited by calling the **submit** method.

Script 8.1 This HTML code creates a form called Form1 that can now be accessed by name with your scripts.

```
File  Edit  Search  Help

<FORM NAME="Form1">
    <INPUT TYPE=BUTTON NAME="Button1" VALUE="OK">
    <INPUT TYPE=BUTTON NAME="Button2" VALUE=
"Cancel">
</FORM>
```

Table 8.1 Methods of the **Form** object.

METHOD	VBSCRIPT
submit	submits the form

Table 8.2 Events of the **Form** object.

EVENT	VBSCRIPT
onSubmit	occurs when the form is submitted

Table 8.3 Form elements and their properties, methods, and events.

ELEMENT	PROPERTIES	METHODS	EVENTS
Button,	form, name, reset,submit	click value	onClick
Checkbox	form, name, value, checked, defaultChecked	click	onClick
Radio	form, name, value, checked	click, focus	onClick
Password	form, name, value, defaultValue	focus, blur, select	
Text, textarea	form, name, value, defaultValue	focus, blur, select	onFocus, onBlur, onChange, onSelect
Select	name, length, options, selectedIndex	focus, blur	onFocus, onBlur, onChange
Hidden	name, value		

Table 8.4 Properties of the **Element** object.

PROPERTY	DESCRIPTION
checked	contains the checked state of a CHECKBOX form element
defaultChecked	contains the default checked value of the CHECKBOX element
defaultValue	contains the default value of the form element
form	refers to the Form object that contains the element
length	contains the number of choices in a SELECT form element
name	contains the name of the form element
options	contains the OPTIONS tags for a SELECT form element
selectedIndex	contains the index of the selected option in a SELECT element
value	contains the value of the form element

Table 8.5 Methods of the **Element** object.

METHOD	DESCRIPTION
blur	removes the focus from the form element
click	simulates a mouse-click on the form element
focus	sets the focus to the form element
select	selects the contents of the form element

THE ELEMENT OBJECT

The **Element** object is a list of all of the form elements—user interface gadgets like radio buttons, checkboxes and text fields—that exist in the current form. Like other lists in the object hierarchy, the **Element** object's list of form elements begins at zero and goes up. What this means is that the first element in the first form is referred to as

forms(0).elements(0)

The second is referred to as

forms(0).elements(1)

and so on.

You can also access form elements by name. If you have a form named **Form1** and a form element named **Button1**, you can access that button more simply as

Form1.Button1

The **Element** object introduces numerous properties, methods, and events, but they are dependent on the type of element: each type of form element supports certain properties, methods, and events. Refer to **Table 8.3, Table 8.4, Table 8.5,** and **Table 8.6** for details.

Table 8.6 Events of the **Element** object.

EVENT	OCCURS WHEN
onBlur	the form element loses the focus
onChange	the value of the element changes
onClick	the element is clicked
onFocus	the form element gets the focus
onSelect	the contents of the form element are selected

USING A COMMAND BUTTON

Command buttons are probably the most often-used form element. A command button is created by setting the **TYPE** attribute of the element to **BUTTON** or **SUBMIT**. Submit command buttons are a special kind of button, and they're covered at the end of this chapter.

A typical command button might look something like **Figure 8.1.** This button was created with the following code:

```
<FORM>

  <INPUT TYPE=BUTTON NAME=
"Button1" VALUE="Click me!">

</FORM>
```

The only major thing you will do with a command button is handle its **onClick** event—the event that occurs when the user clicks the button with the mouse.

To use a command button:

1. Create a new, blank HTML document and save the file as button.html

2. Add a form section within the body section, as shown in **Script 8.2.**

3. Now you must write some VBScript that will handle the event that occurs when the user clicks the button. Add the script section shown in **Script 8.3.**

4. Save the file and load it in your browser.

Figure 8.2 When you click the form button, an alert dialog will display information about the browser.

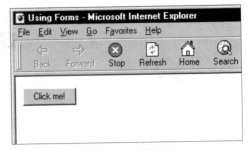

Figure 8.1 A typical command button.

Script 8.2 Creating a simple form button.

```
File  Edit  Search  Help
<HTML>
<HEAD><TITLE>Using Forms</TITLE></HEAD>

<BODY BGCOLOR="#FFFFFF">

<FORM>
  <INPUT TYPE=BUTTON NAME="Button1" VALUE=
"Display info">
</FORM>

</BODY>
</HTML>
```

Script 8.3 This event handler will be triggered when the user clicks the command button.

```
File  Edit  Search  Help
<HTML>
<HEAD><TITLE>Using Forms</TITLE></HEAD>

<BODY BGCOLOR="#FFFFFF">

<FORM>
  <INPUT TYPE=BUTTON NAME="Button1" VALUE=
"Display info">
</FORM>

<SCRIPT LANGUAGE="VBSCRIPT">
<!--
  Sub Button1_onClick
    MyMessage = "Your browser is " &
Navigator.appName & "!"
    alert MyMessage
  End Sub
-->
</SCRIPT>

</BODY>
</HTML>
```

USING A COMMAND BUTTON

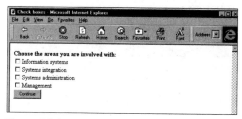

Figure 8.3 A group of check boxes with a single command button.

Script 8.4 Create a list of check boxes.

```
File  Edit  Search  Help
<HTML>
<HEAD><TITLE>Check boxes</TITLE></HEAD>

<BODY BGCOLOR="#FFFFFF">

<FORM NAME="Form1">
  <B>Choose the areas you are involved
with:</B>
  <BR><INPUT TYPE=CHECKBOX NAME="chkIS">
Information systems
  <BR><INPUT TYPE=CHECKBOX NAME="chkSI">
Systems integration
  <BR><INPUT TYPE=CHECKBOX NAME="chkSA">
Systems administration
  <BR><INPUT TYPE=CHECKBOX NAME="chkMgmt">
Management
</FORM>

</BODY>
</HTML>
```

Script 8.5 You can combine form elements, in this case check boxes with a single command button.

```
File  Edit  Search  Help
  <BR><INPUT TYPE=CHECKBOX NAME="chkSI">
Systems integration
  <BR><INPUT TYPE=CHECKBOX NAME="chkSA">
Systems administration
  <BR><INPUT TYPE=CHECKBOX NAME="chkMgmt">
Management

  <BR><INPUT TYPE=BUTTON NAME="Button1"
VALUE="Continue">
</FORM>

</BODY>
</HTML>
```

USING CHECK BOXES

Check boxes are small square boxes that allow the user to make choices. If a check box is checked off (denoted by a little check mark in the square box), that option is chosen. Check boxes are not grouped in any way, so it is possible to have a large number of check boxes in a form with any number of checked or unchecked boxes. You can combine check boxes with command buttons, and once you gather information from the user, you can react to it as well.

In the following steps, you first create a group of check boxes and a command button, then add a script that reacts to the user's selection.

To create a group of check boxes:

1. Create a new, blank HTML file and save it as **checkbox.html**

2. Add a form section to the body section, as shown in **Script 8.4.**

2. Add a command button to the form section, as shown in **Script 8.5.**

3. Save the file and load in your browser. The result should resemble **Figure.8.3.**

Now you can use an event handler to react to the user.

(Continued on the next page.)

Tip:

- You can select a check box by default using the following code:

  `<FORM>`

  `<INPUT TYPE=CHECKBOX NAME="Box1" CHECKED>` name of box

  `</FORM>`

USING CHECK BOXES

(Continued from the previous page.)

To respond to the user's selection:

1. Place the code shown in **Script 8.6** above the body section.

2. Save the file and load it in your browser. The result should resemble **Figure 8.4.**

Note:

■ Remember that you can copy the code for these projects from

http://www.internet-nexus.com/vbvqs

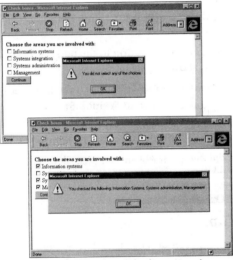

Figure 8.4 The alert dialog box correctly identifies which check boxes are checked, regardless of which combination of boxes is checked.

Script 8.6 This event handler first determines which check boxes are checked and then displays the appropriate message.

```
File  Edit  Search  Help

<HTML>
<HEAD><TITLE>Check boxes</TITLE></HEAD>

<SCRIPT LANGUAGE="VBSCRIPT">
<!--
  Sub Button1_onClick
    Dim Selections, Count
    Count = 0
    Selections = ""

    If Form1.Elements(0).checked = 1 Then
      Selections = "Information Systems"
      Count = Count + 1
    End If

    If Form1.Elements(1).checked = 1 Then
      If Count <> 0 Then
        Selections = Selections & ", "
      End If
      Selections = Selections & "Systems
integration"
      Count = Count + 1
    End If

    If Form1.Elements(2).checked = 1 Then
      If Count <> 0 Then
        Selections = Selections & ", "
      End If
      Selections = Selections & "Systems
administration"
      Count = Count + 1
    End If

    If Form1.Elements(3).checked = 1 Then
      If Count <> 0 Then
        Selections = Selections & ", "
      End If
      Selections = Selections & "Management"
      Count = Count + 1
    End If

    If Selections = "" Then
      alert "You did not select any of the
choices"
    Else
      alert "You checked the following: " &
Selections
    End If

  End Sub
-->
</SCRIPT>

<BODY BGCOLOR="#FFFFFF">
```

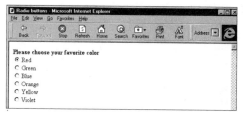

Figure 8.5 Radio buttons are grouped and only one can be checked at a time.

Script 8.7 Each radio button in a group will have the same name, as set by the **NAME** attribute, in this case **rdoColor**. Only one button in a group can be selected at a time. The command button allows you to act on the user's selection.

```
File  Edit  Search  Help

<HTML>
<HEAD><TITLE>Radio buttons</TITLE></HEAD>

<BODY BGCOLOR="#FFFFFF">

<FORM NAME="Form1">
  <B>Please choose your favorite color</B>
  <BR><INPUT TYPE=RADIO NAME="rdoColor"
VALUE="White" CHECKED> White
  <BR><INPUT TYPE=RADIO NAME="rdoColor"
VALUE="Red"> Red
  <BR><INPUT TYPE=RADIO NAME="rdoColor"
VALUE="Green"> Green
  <BR><INPUT TYPE=RADIO NAME="rdoColor"
VALUE="Blue"> Blue
  <BR><INPUT TYPE=RADIO NAME="rdoColor"
VALUE="Magenta"> Magenta
  <BR><INPUT TYPE=RADIO NAME="rdoColor"
VALUE="Yellow"> Yellow
  <BR><INPUT TYPE=RADIO NAME="rdoColor"
VALUE="Purple"> Purple
  <P><INPUT TYPE=BUTTON NAME="Button1"
VALUE="Ready">
</FORM>

</BODY>
</HTML>
```

Figure 8.6 Each time you click the command button, the background color changes to match the selected color.

Using Radio Buttons

Radio buttons are very similar to check boxes—a group of buttons from which the user can select a range of choices. Unlike check boxes, however, radio buttons are *mutually exclusive*, that is, only one radio button in a group can be checked at a time, and choosing one button in a group "unchecks" any other. If you want the user to choose only one option as shown in **Figure 8.5,** the radio button is an ideal tool to use.

In the following steps, you create a Web page that allows the user to control the background color.

To use radio buttons:

1. Create a new, blank HTML file and save it as radio.html

2. Add a form section within the body section, as shown in **Script 8.7.**

3. Now, add the event handler for the command button above the body section, as shown in **Script 8.8.**

4. Save the file and check it out. The result should resemble **Figure 8.6.**

Script 8.8 This event handler determines the **VALUE** attribute of the checked radio button and uses it to set the background color of the document.

```
File  Edit  Search  Help

<HTML>
<HEAD><TITLE>Radio buttons</TITLE></HEAD>

<SCRIPT LANGUAGE="VBSCRIPT">
<!--
  Sub Button1_onClick
    For X = 0 to Form1.elements.count - 2
      If Form1.elements(x).checked = 1 Then
        Document.bgColor =
Form1.elements(x).value
      End If
    Next
  End Sub
-->
</SCRIPT>

<BODY BGCOLOR="#FFFFFF">
```

USING A TEXT BOX

A *text box* allows the user to enter a single line of text into a form. **Figure 8.7** shows a typical form text box.

The text box supports four events: onFocus, onBlur, onChange, and onSelect. The onFocus event occurs when the user clicks in the text box or tabs over to it so they can enter some text. The onBlur event occurs when the user tabs out of the text box or clicks elsewhere. The onChange event occurs when the user changes the contents of the text box. And, finally, the onSelect event occurs when the user selects some text in the text box.

To use a text box:

1. Create a new, blank HTML file and save it as **textbox.html**

2. Add the HTML code to the body section, as shown in **Script 8.9.**

3. Add event handlers for the four events in the body section, as shown in **Script 8.10.**

4. Save the file and view it in your browser. Test the text box. Select the text, click the button, click the text box after you've clicked the button, and enter text in the text box. Sometimes you will have to tab out of the text box for the event to register. The result should resemble **Figure 8.8.**

Figure 8.8 The text box supports some pretty cool events.

Figure 8.7 A typical form text box. You can set default text in the box using the **VALUE** attribute.

Script 8.9 In creating the text box, you control the size and length of both the box and an acceptable entry.

```
File  Edit  Search  Help

<HTML>
<HEAD><TITLE>Text box</TITLE></HEAD>

<BODY BGCOLOR="#FFFFFF">

<FORM>Go ahead, type something. I dare you:
   <BR><INPUT NAME="AlGore"
         VALUE="<<<Please type something here>>>"
         TYPE=TEXT SIZE=50 MAXLENGTH=50>
   <P><INPUT NAME="Button1" TYPE=BUTTON
VALUE="OK">
</FORM>

</BODY>
</HTML>
```

Script 8.10 This script contains event handlers for the **onBlur, onFocus, onChange**, and **onSelect** events.

```
File  Edit  Search  Help

<HTML>
<HEAD><TITLE>Text box</TITLE></HEAD>

SCRIPT LANGUAGE="VBSCRIPT">
<!--
   Sub AlGore_onFocus
      alert "Hey! Get out of that text box!"
   End Sub

   Sub AlGore_onBlur
      alert "Where are you going? Did I offend
you?"
   End Sub

   Sub AlGore_onChange
      alert "You dare change my text???"
   End Sub

   Sub AlGore_onSelect
      alert "Sure, select it if you must!"
   End Sub
-->
</SCRIPT>

<BODY BGCOLOR="#FFFFFF">
```

Figure 8.9 Text areas offer a way to collect larger amounts of information from your users.

Script 8.11 The **COLS** attribute determines the width of the text area in characters. The default is **40**. The **ROWS** attribute determines the height of the text area in rows of text. The default value is **4**. Unlike most of the other form elements, the text area element has its own tag, **<TEXTAREA>**.

```
File  Edit  Search  Help

<HTML>
<HEAD><TITLE>Text area</TITLE></HEAD>

<BODY BGCOLOR="#FFFFFF">
<FORM NAME="Form1">
   Please enter your name:
   <BR><INPUT TYPE=TEXT NAME="txtName" SIZE=50>
   <P>Please tell us a little about yourself:
   <BR><TEXTAREA NAME="taAbout" COLS=60
ROWS=5></TEXTAREA>
</FORM>

</BODY>
</HTML>
```

Script 8.12 Use the **Window** object's **onLoad** event handler to make sure the text area gets the focus.

```
File  Edit  Search  Help

<HTML>
<HEAD><TITLE>Text area</TITLE></HEAD>

<SCRIPT LANGUAGE="VBSCRIPT">
<!--
   Sub Window_onLoad
      Form1.elements(1).focus
   End Sub
-->
</SCRIPT>

<BODY BGCOLOR="#FFFFFF">
<FORM NAME="Form1">
   Please enter your name:
   <BR><INPUT TYPE=TEXT NAME="txtName" SIZE=50>
   <P>Please tell us a little about yourself:
```

USING A TEXT AREA

A *text area* is simply a big text box. It allows you to specify multiple lines of text in addition to a width. If the user adds more text than the size of the text box allows, scroll bars will appear so the user can keep typing. **Figure 8.9** shows a typical text area.

Like the text box, the text area supports the onFocus, onBlur, onChange, and onSelect events. The last section shows how to work with these events, but it's good to know that you can achieve the same results using methods instead. In the following steps, you will take a look at one of these methods, since they all work the same way.

To use a text area:

1. Create a new, blank HTML file and save it as **textarea.html**

2. Add a form inside the body section that contains a text box and a text area, as shown in **Script 8.11.**

3. Typically, the first form element will receive the focus when the page loads. The text area's **focus** method, however, sets the focus to the text area when the page loads. Add the script section shown in **Script 8.12** before the body section.

4. Save the file and view it in your browser. The result should resemble **Figure 8.10.**

Figure 8.10 When the page loads, the focus will be in the text area, not the text box as usual.

95

USING A LIST BOX

The form *select control* is really just a Windows list box, and is sometimes mistakenly referred to as a "menu." It's not actually a menu in the Windows sense of the word, but a user interface gadget that presents a list of options to the user. **Figure 8.11** shows a form select control.

When using a select control with VBScript, you can handle the onFocus, onBlur, and onChange events. The onFocus event occurs when the control receives the user focus. The onBlur event occurs when the user moves the focus out of the control. OnChange occurs when you change the selected option.

To use a select control:

1. Create a blank, new HTML file and save it as **select.html**

2. Add a form section as shown in **Script 8.13**.

3. Now you need to handle the event that occurs when the command button is clicked, as shown in **Script 8.14.**

4. Save your file and load it in your browser. The result should resemble **Figure 8.12**.

Note:

- The **VALUE** attribute lists the value that will be sent to a CGI application.

- The **VALUE** attribute can be different from the text you display in the list box. If the text is the same, you can leave out the **VALUE** attribute altogether and save yourself some typing.

Figure 8.12 I guess they're all fine automobiles. You can judge the user's choice as you see fit.

Figure 8.11 The select control emulates a Windows list box.

Script 8.13 The select control uses a HTML tag, **<SELECT>**, to enclose each of the list box entries. A list of **<OPTION>** tags identifies each entry. The **SELECTED** attribute in one of the **<OPTION>** tags makes that entry the default choice.

```
File  Edit  Search  Help

<HTML>
<HEAD><TITLE>List box</TITLE></HEAD>

<BODY BGCOLOR="#FFFFFF">

<FORM NAME="Form1">Please select a make:
  <BR><SELECT NAME="Select1" SIZE=10
VALUE="Selection">
    <OPTION SELECTED>Acura
    <OPTION>Audi
    <OPTION>BMW
    <OPTION>Buick
    <OPTION>Cadillac
    <OPTION>Chevrolet
    <OPTION>Chrysler
    <OPTION>Dodge
    <OPTION>Ford
    <OPTION>Honda
  </SELECT>
  <P><INPUT TYPE=BUTTON NAME="Button1"
VALUE="Continue">
</FORM>
</BODY>
</HTML>
```

Script 8.14 This code gets the text that follows the selected item in the select control and displays it in an alert dialog box.

```
File  Edit  Search  Help

<HTML>
<HEAD><TITLE>List box</TITLE></HEAD>

<SCRIPT LANGUAGE="VBSCRIPT">
<!--
    Sub Button1_onClick
        alert("The " &
Form1.Select1.options(selectedIndex).text & _
            " is a fine automobile.")
    End Sub
-->
</SCRIPT>

<BODY BGCOLOR="#FFFFFF">
```

Script 8.15 This script posts a form to a CGI application.

```
File  Edit  Search  Help

<HTML>
<HEAD><TITLE>Submitting a form</TITLE></HEAD>
<BODY BGCOLOR="#FFFFFF">

<FORM NAME="Form1" METHOD="Post" ACTION="/cgi-
bin/getinfo.exe">
Please enter your data:
  <FONT FACE="Courier New">
  <P> Name: <INPUT TYPE=TEXT SIZE=30>
  <BR>Email: <INPUT TYPE=TEXT SIZE=30>
  <P><INPUT TYPE=SUBMIT>  <INPUT
TYPE=RESET>
  </FONT>
</FORM>
```

Figure 8.13 This form will be submitted to a Web server CGI application.

SUBMITTING A FORM

Usually, you use a form to post information to a CGI application running on a Web server. A CGI application takes the information from the form, processes it and returns output, usually HTML text, back to the browser. While we can't cover CGI applications in depth here, it is worth noting what you can do with VBScript when you are submitting a form.

A form that posts to a CGI application might look something like **Script 8.15.** The **METHOD** attribute in the **<FORM>** tag indicates that the values of the form elements will be posted to a CGI application. The **ACTION** attribute identifies the CGI application, which in this case is a fictional program called **getinfo.exe** that resides in the cgi-bin directory on the Web server. There are two command buttons here as well, and they are special case command buttons, as identified by their **TYPE** attributes. The first one, submit, causes the form to be sent to the CGI application. The second one, reset, erases the data in any form elements when clicked so the user can re-enter all the data.

So, where does VBScript come into play? Well, VBScript offers a method and an event that aid with form submission. The **submit** method is designed to force a form submission using VBScript code. This means you can submit a form when you wish, not just in response to the user clicking the submit button. The event, called **onSubmit**, occurs when the user clicks the submit button. The **onSubmit** event allows you to process VBScript code that executes before the data is sent, allowing you to do form validation.Before we move on to validating form data with **onSubmit**, let's take a look at forcing the submission of a form.

(Continued on the next page.)

(Continued from the previous page.)

To submit a form:

1. Create a new, blank HTML file and save it as submit.html

2. Add the form section above the body section, as shown in **Script 8.16.**

3. Add the script section shown in **Script 8.17** above the body section to handle the command button's **onClick** event.

4. Save the file and view it in your browser. The results should resemble **Figure 8.14.**

Note:

■ The form in this example won't actually get submitted, because the CGI application used in this example doesn't actually exist. If you are using a CGI application supplied by your ISP, company, or co-worker, however, this type of confirmation is easily accomplished with VBScript: just substitute the correct name of the CGI application you are using.

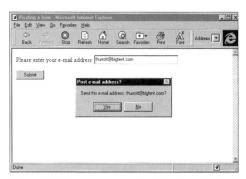

Figure 8.14 If the user clicks "Yes," the form is submitted. If not, the user returns to the form and can begin editing immediately, without clicking on the form box.

Script 8.16 This form section defines a text box and a command button that will work like a submit button with one additional advantage: you can submit the data when you want to after the user clicks the button.

```
File  Edit  Search  Help
<HTML>
<HEAD><TITLE>Submitting a form</TITLE></HEAD>

<BODY BGCOLOR="#FFFFFF">

<FORM NAME="Form1" METHOD="Post" ACTION=
"/cgi-bin/getinfo.exe">
   Please enter your e-mail address:
   <INPUT TYPE=TEST SIZE=40 NAME="txtEmail">
   <P><INPUT TYPE=BUTTON VALUE="Submit"
NAME="Button1">
</FORM>

</BODY>
</HTML>
```

Script 8.17 This event handler shows users the text they inputted and makes sure that's what they want to send.

```
File  Edit  Search  Help
<HTML>
<HEAD><TITLE>Submitting a form</TITLE></HEAD>

<SCRIPT LANGUAGE="VBSCRIPT">
<!--
Sub Button1_onClick
    If MsgBox("Send this e-mail address: " &
Form1.txtEmail.value & _
            "?", 4, "Post e-mail address?")
= 6 Then
       Form1.submit
    Else
       Form1.txtEmail.focus
    End If
End Sub
-->
</SCRIPT>

<BODY BGCOLOR="#FFFFFF">

<FORM NAME="Form1" METHOD="Post" ACTION="/cgi-
bin/getinfo.exe">
```

Script 8.18 A table-based form lets you line up elements.

```
File  Edit  Search  Help

<HTML>
<HEAD><TITLE>Validating a form</TITLE></HEAD>

<BODY BGCOLOR="#FFFFFF">

<FORM NAME="Form1" METHOD="Post" ACTION=
"/cgi-bin/getinfo.exe">
  <TABLE WIDTH=400 CELLPADDING=0 CELLSPACING=0
COLS=3 BORDER=0>
    <TR>
      <TD ALIGN=RIGHT VALIGN=TOP
WIDTH=100>Name:</TD>
      <TD WIDTH=25><BR></TD>
      <TD ALIGN=LEFT VALIGN=TOP WIDTH=475>
      <INPUT TYPE=TEST SIZE=40
NAME="txtName">
      </TD>
    </TR>
    <TR>
      <TD ALIGN=RIGHT VALIGN=TOP>E-mail:</TD>
      <TD><BR></TD>
      <TD ALIGN=LEFT VALIGN=TOP>
      <INPUT TYPE=TEST SIZE=40
NAME="txtEmail">
      </TD>
    </TR>
    <TR>
      <TD ALIGN=RIGHT VALIGN=TOP>Phone:</TD>
      <TD><BR></TD>
      <TD ALIGN=LEFT VALIGN=TOP>
      <INPUT TYPE=TEST SIZE=40 NAME=
"txtPhone">
      </TD>
    </TR>
    <TR>
      <TD ALIGN=LEFT VALIGN=TOP WIDTH=600
COLSPAN=3>
      <BR><INPUT TYPE=BUTTON VALUE="Submit"
NAME="Button1">
      </TD>
    </TR>
  </TABLE>
</FORM>

</BODY>
</HTML>
```

VALIDATING A FORM

Now that you're familiar with the way VBScript interacts with forms, you can move on to the number one reason to script your forms: data validation. *Data validation* means that you are verifying data sent to the Web server before it gets delivered. Before VBScript, the only way to validate data entered with a form was with the CGI application itself. This is inefficient, however: if you can validate the data before it gets to the CGI application, the whole process will move faster. And speed is, after all, the number one problem with the Internet right now.

The way you validate data depends on the type of data you are asking the user for. The simplest form of data validation is to make sure that every field in a form is filled in.

Now, data validation is a vast subject, and we can't cover every possible situation here. In the following steps, however, you will develop a nice data validation routine to check that e-mail addresses are valid.

To validate a form:

1. Create a new, blank HTML file and save it as **validate.html**

2. Add the form section shown in **Script 8.18** to the body section.

(Continued on the next page.)

VALIDATING A FORM

(Continued from the previous page.)

3. Now, add the simple data validation script section above the body section, as shown in **Script 8.19**.

4. Load the file in your browser and play with the form. Your results should resemble **Figure 8.15**.

At this point, you have a form that will at least check to make sure all of the fields have some kind of data entered in them. In this case, though, you need to add to the code to check for the special characters in an e-mail address.

To check for special characters:

1. Open validate.html in your HTML editor.

2. Modify the script section's event handler to check for @ and . characters in the e-mail address. **Script 8.20** shows the completed script section with the newly added script highlighted.

3. Save the file and give it a whirl. The result should resemble **Figure 8.16**.

Note:

■ Even this validation is not perfect: You could enter @. as the e-mail address and it would work. Still, it's better than no validation at all, and the complexity of the script should give you some insights into the problems of data validation.

■ Remember all of these code samples are available at:

http://www.internet-nexus.com/vbvqs

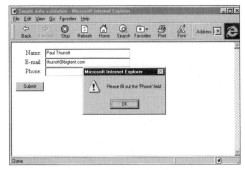

Figure 8.15 The event handler for the command button ensures that every field has at least something written in it.

Script 8.19 The following code makes sure that every field in the form shown in **Figure 8.15** is filled out. This is a valiant attempt, but it is lacking in some areas. For example, no actual validation is occurring: as long as the user has entered something—anything—in each field, the form will be submitted.

```
File  Edit  Search  Help

<HTML>
<HEAD><TITLE>Validating a form</TITLE></HEAD>

<SCRIPT LANGUAGE="VBSCRIPT">
<!--
   Sub Button1_onClick
     If Form1.elements(0).value <> "" Then
       If Form1.elements(1).value <> "" Then
         If Form1.elements(2).value <> "" Then
           Form1.submit
         Else
           alert "Please fill out the 'Phone' field"
           Form1.elements(2).focus
         End If
       Else
         alert "Please fill out the 'E-mail' field"
         Form1.elements(1).focus
       End If
     Else
       alert "Please fill out the 'Name' field"
       Form1.elements(0).focus
     End If
   End Sub
-->
</SCRIPT>

<BODY BGCOLOR="#FFFFFF">

<FORM NAME="Form1" METHOD="Post" ACTION=
"/cgi-bin/getinfo.exe">
  <TABLE WIDTH=400 CELLPADDING=0 CELLSPACING=0 COLS=3
BORDER=0>
```

Script 8.20 Add the highlighted sections of script to your event handler to add e-mail validation.

```
File  Edit  Search  Help

<HTML>
<HEAD><TITLE>Validating a form</TITLE></HEAD>

<BODY BGCOLOR="#FFFFFF">

<SCRIPT LANGUAGE="VBSCRIPT">
<!--
  Sub Button1_onClick
    If Form1.elements(0).value <> "" Then
      If Form1.elements(1).value <> "" Then
        If Form1.elements(2).value <> "" Then
          ' OK, all of the fields have some value
entered.
          ' Now check e-mail address
          ' First check for @ character
          If InStr(Form1.elements(1).value, "@") <>
0 Then
            If InStr(Form1.elements(1).value, ".")
<> 0 Then
              Form1.submit
            Else
              alert "Your e-mail address has no
'.' character."
              Form1.elements(1).focus
            End If
          Else
            alert "Your e-mail address has no '@'
character."
            Form1.elements(1).focus
          End If
        Else
          alert "Please fill out the 'Phone' field"
          Form1.elements(2).focus
        End If
      Else
        alert "Please fill out the 'E-mail' field"
        Form1.elements(1).focus
      End If
    Else
      alert "Please fill out the 'Name' field"
      Form1.elements(0).focus
    End If
  End Sub
-->
</SCRIPT>

</BODY>

<FORM NAME="Form1" METHOD="Post" ACTION=
"/cgi-bin/getinfo.exe">
```

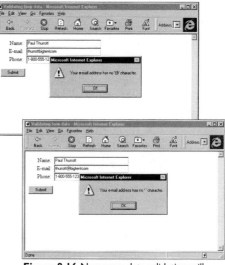

Figure 8.16 Now your data validation will check for the @ and . characters in the e-mail address.

ActiveX and ActiveX Controls

9

Table 9.1 ActiveX technologies.

TECHNOLOGY	DESCRIPTION
ActiveX controls	lightweight controls and user interface widgets
ActiveX Documents	allow Word, Excel, and other documents to display in Web browsers
Active Scripting	VBScript and JScript—used to add interactivity and to control ActiveX controls
Java applets	small controls and user interface widgets written with Java
Java Virtual Machine	an extension to the operating system that allows Java applets to run
ActiveX Server Framework	ActiveX extensions for the Web server

Microsoft created VBScript to facilitate the use of ActiveX controls. *ActiveX* is a set of related technologies created by Microsoft that enables Web designers and developers to create interactive, multimedia content for the World Wide Web. The ActiveX technologies also include tools for programmers. Besides VBScript, other ActiveX technologies include JScript (Microsoft's version of JavaScript), ActiveX controls, the ActiveX Server Framework (for ActiveX scripting and programming on the Web server), ActiveX Documents (so you can view Word, Excel, and other documents right in your browser), and the Java Virtual Machine, which allows the user to view Java applets and applications. **Table 9.1** summarizes the technologies known as ActiveX.

This chapter introduces ActiveX and ActiveX controls and some of the more interesting things you can do with them. While intimidating on first blush, you'll find these technologies easy to use, and well worth the effort to learn.

WHAT ARE ACTIVEX CONTROLS?

ActiveX controls are simply little programs you can run inside of a Web browser or other program. They typically take the form of user interface widgets like buttons, text boxes, and scrolling text marquees. There are also ActiveX controls specially created to provide specific functionality like a stock ticker and a control that displays Macromedia Shockwave animations. The cool thing about ActiveX controls is that they are small and fast, and, unlike Java applets, can be downloaded to your computer so you can use them again. If you visit a Web site that has an ActiveX control, you can choose to download the control. That way, the site will come up instantaneously the next time you visit.

Today, there are more than 1,000 ActiveX controls available commercially, which were created using a variety of programming languages. Using an ActiveX control in your Web pages, however, does not require any programming experience, just a little VBScript. And that's the beauty of ActiveX, really. Nonprogrammers can add these elegant controls to Web pages easily.

Note:

■ Microsoft Internet Explorer 3.0 and 4.0 come with a number of ActiveX controls that install automatically with the browser. Microsoft also provides other ActiveX controls that you can download from its Web site. The ActiveX Controls Gallery contains numerous controls from other companies as well, and they're all available for free. Check out:

http://www.microsoft.com/activex/gallery/

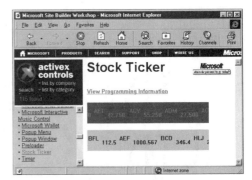

Figure 9.1 A stock ticker ActiveX control.

Figure 9.2 The ActiveX Control Gallery on the Microsoft Web site offers numerous free controls.

Figure 9.3 Java applets, like ActiveX controls, are typically user interface widgets seen running in a browser.

Table 9.2 Common attributes.

ATTRIBUTE	CLASSID VALUE
ID	the name of the control; how you will reference the control with script
WIDTH	the width of the control in pixels (only needed for visual controls)
HEIGHT	the height of the control in pixels (only needed for visual controls)
CLASSID	the "class identifier," a string of letters and characters that uniquely identifies each type of control

Script 9.1 This script adds a Label control to a Web page, embedded in HTML.

```
File  Edit  Search  Help

<HTML>
<HEAD><TITLE>Angled text demo</TITLE></HEAD>

<BODY BGCOLOR="#FFFFFF">

<P>The following ActiveX control...

<OBJECT ID="IeLabel1" WIDTH=137 HEIGHT=15
        CLASSID="CLSID:99B42120-6EC7-11CF-A6C7-
00AA00A47DD2">
   <PARAM NAME="Caption" VALUE="<<Hello
there!>>">
</OBJECT>

 was brought to you by Microsoft.
</BODY>

</HTML>
```

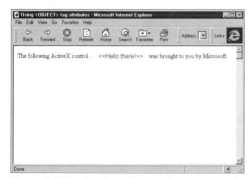

Figure 9.4 Your first ActiveX control.

INSERTING AN ACTIVEX CONTROL

You add ActiveX controls to your Web pages by inserting a set of <OBJECT> tags in the HTML. The <OBJECT> tag can take a number of attributes and parameters. You can also add parameters using <PARAM> tags inside the <OBJECT> tags. ActiveX controls, like other objects, have properties, methods, and events that you can access through scripting.

When adding ActiveX controls to your Web pages, there are only a couple of attributes that you need to use, as shown in **Table 9.2**.

To insert an ActiveX control:

1. Create a new, blank HTML file and save it as **object.html**

2. Add the code shown in **Script 9.1**. This script adds a couple of lines of HTML and an ActiveX Label control with numerous attributes.

3. Save the file and view it in your browser. The result should resemble **Figure 9.4**.

Tips:

- ActiveX Control Pad (see Chapter 10) offers an easier way to get CLASSID values and <PARAM> tags for each control.

- **Table 9.3** lists the CLASSIDs for some of the common controls that Microsoft provides for free with Internet Explorer 3.0.

Table 9.3 Common CLASSIDs

CONTROL	CLASSID VALUE
Label	CLSID:99B42120-6EC7-11CF-A6C7-00AA00A47DD2
Marquee	CLSID:1A4DA620-6217-11CF-BE62-0080C72EDD2D
Menu	CLSID:52DFAE60-CEBF-11CF-A3A9-00A0C9034920
Popup menu	CLSID:7823A620-9DD9-11CF-A662-00AA00C066D2
Popup window	CLSID: A23D7C20-CABA-11CF-A5D4-00AA00A47DD2
Stock Ticker	CLSID: 0CA4A620-8E3D-11CF-A3A9-00A0C9034920
Timer	CLSID:59CCB4A0-727D-11CF-AC36-00AA00A47DD2

ADDING ACTIVEX CONTROLS TO A USER'S COMPUTER

The CODEBASE attribute of the <OBJECT> tag allows you to specify a place where an ActiveX control can be found on the Internet. This way, if the user accessing your page doesn't have the control, it can automatically be downloaded to the user's machine as the page loads. You should always use the CODEBASE attribute in your <OBJECT> tags if you want to ensure that your users see your pages correctly. Remember: Once users download the control, they will not have to download it again. And most ActiveX controls are pretty small, so they don't take too long to download.

To install an ActiveX control on a user's computer:

1. Create a new blank HTML file and save it as codebase.html

2. Use the script shown in **Script 9.2** to add a MCSILabel control to the page. The code for this control includes the **CODEBASE** attribute, which allows users to download the control if they don't already have it.

3. Save the file and load it in your browser. The result should resemble **Figure 9.5**.

Tip:

■ You can find out more about the MCSI Label and other ActiveX controls at Microsoft's ActiveX Control Gallery Web site:

http://www.microsoft.com/activex/gallery/

Script 9.2 This script adds a new label control called **MCSILabel** that offers a couple of improvements over the standard label: it can have an optional 3D style with a variety of beveled edge styles.

```
File  Edit  Search  Help

<HTML>
<HEAD><TITLE>Using CODEBASE</TITLE></HEAD>

<BODY BGCOLOR="#FFFFFF">

OBJECT ID="Label3D" WIDTH=150 HEIGHT=100
  CLASSID="CLSID:40F07A91-8E6F-11D0-8A0A-
00A0C90C9B67"
  CODEBASE="mcsilabl.cab#version1,0,0,45">
    <PARAM NAME="Text" VALUE="Cool 3D Label">
    <PARAM NAME="Angle" VALUE="0">
    <PARAM NAME="BorderStyle" VALUE="0">
</OBJECT>

</BODY>

</HTML>
```

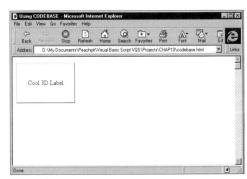

Figure 9.5 The MCSILabel provides a 3D border.

```
Sub ControlID_EventName()

  'VBScript code to handle the event

End Sub
```

Figure 9.6 ActiveX control event handlers take this general form.

```
<SCRIPT LANGUAGE="VBSCRIPT">

<!--

  Sub Label1_Click()

    alert "Hey, you clicked the label!"

  End Sub

-->

</SCRIPT>
```

Figure 9.7 To handle the Click event for a Label control named **Label1**, you might write code like this.

SCRIPTING AN ACTIVEX CONTROL EVENT

ActiveX controls, like other objects, have properties, methods, and events. Control properties are set with the <PARAM> tags you embed inside the <OBJECT> tags. Methods are particular to each control and will be covered on a control-by-control basis in the upcoming pages of this chapter. Finally, ActiveX control events work just like their Object Scripting Model counterparts: each control has a list of events that can occur to it; you respond to these events with VBScript event handlers.

One little difference between an ActiveX control event and an event for an object in the Internet Explorer Scripting Object Model (SOM) is that ActiveX control events do not start with **on.** An object in the SOM might have events like **onClick** and **onMouseOver** whereas ActiveX controls have events such as **Click** and **MouseOver.**

In the following steps you handle the **Click** event for the **Label** control and use it to change the angle of the text message it displays.

(Continued on the next page.)

(Continued from the previous page.)

To script an ActiveX control event:

1. Create a new, blank HTML file and save the file as **axevent.html**

2. Add the code shown in **Script 9.3** inside the body section to insert an ActiveX Label control.

3. Now, you will handle the event that occurs when the user clicks the label. The script section shown in **Script 9.4** will rotate the text message each time the label is clicked by changing the control's **Angle** property. Add this script section above the body section.

4. Save the file and load it in your browser. Each time you click the label, the text will rotate, as shown in **Figure 9.8.**

Note:

- Don't forget that you can copy all of the code for these examples from:

  http://www.internet-nexus.com/vbvqs

Figure 9.8 Every time you click on the label, the text rotates.

Script 9.3 Insert an ActiveX Label control.

```
File  Edit  Search  Help

<HTML>
<HEAD><TITLE>ActiveX Event</TITLE></HEAD>

<BODY BGCOLOR="#FFFFFF">

<OBJECT ID="Label1" WIDTH=300 HEIGHT=240
  CLASSID="CLSID:99B42120-6EC7-11CF-A6C7-
00AA00A47DD2">
    <PARAM NAME="Caption" VALUE="Angled text
with the Label control!">
      <PARAM NAME="FontName" VALUE="Times New
Roman">
      <PARAM NAME="FontSize" VALUE="14">
</OBJECT>


</SCRIPT>
</BODY>
</HTML>
```

Script 9.4 This event handler rotates the text 36 degrees every time the label is clicked.

```
File  Edit  Search  Help

<HTML>
<HEAD><TITLE>ActiveX Event</TITLE></HEAD>

<BODY BGCOLOR="#FFFFFF">

<OBJECT ID="Label1" WIDTH=300 HEIGHT=240
  CLASSID="CLSID:99B42120-6EC7-11CF-A6C7-
00AA00A47DD2">
    <PARAM NAME="Caption" VALUE="Angled text
with the Label control!">
      <PARAM NAME="FontName" VALUE="Times New
Roman">
      <PARAM NAME="FontSize" VALUE="14">
</OBJECT>


<SCRIPT LANGUAGE="VBSCRIPT">
<!--
   Sub Label1_Click()
     If Label1.Angle <= 324 Then
       Label1.Angle = Label1.Angle + 36
     Else
       Label1.Angle = 0
     End If
   End Sub
-->
</SCRIPT>
</BODY>
</HTML>
```

Table 9.4 Properties of the Label ActiveX control.

PROPERTY	WHAT IT DOES
Alignment	determines how text is aligned in the control using the values shown in Table 9.5
Angle	shows the angle of the text, in degrees
Backstyle	determines whether the background is transparent or opaque using the values shown in Table 9.6
Caption	shows the text message displayed by the control
FontBold	determines whether the text is bold
FontItalic	determines whether the text is italicized
FontName	determines the font used to display the text message
FontSize	determines the size of the font, in points
FontStrikeout	determines whether the text has a line through it
FontUnderline	determines whether the text is underlined

Table 9.5 Value of the **Alignment** property of the Label ActiveX control.

VALUE	ALIGNMENT
0	aligned to left (horizontal) and to top (vertical)
1	centered (horizontal) and to top (vertical)
2	aligned to right (horizontal) and to top (vertical)
3	aligned to left (horizontal) and centered (vertical)
4	centered (horizontal) and centered (vertical)
5	aligned to right (horizontal) and centered (vertical)
6	aligned to left (horizontal) and to bottom (vertical)
7	centered (horizontal) and to bottom (vertical)
8	aligned to right (horizontal) and to bottom (vertical)

Table 9.6 Value of the **Backstyle** property of the Label ActiveX control.

VALUE	ALIGNMENT
0	transparent
1	opaque

Table 9.7 Methods of the Label ActiveX control

METHOD	WHAT IT DOES
AboutBox	displays an About box for the control

USING THE LABEL CONTROL

The **Label** control introduces the properties, methods, and events shown in the **Table 9.4** and **Table 9.5.** The properties are all set with <PARAM> tags, so if you want to set the Caption property when the page loads, add the following code within the <OBJECT> and </OBJECT> tags for the **Label** control:

> <PARAM NAME="Caption" VALUE="This will appear as the text message!">

As mentioned previously, the **Label** control displays a text message to the browser window. The beauty of this control, though, is that it also responds to mouse-clicks and can be rotated at will. Since it is an ActiveX control, you can change the text it displays however you wish after the page loads, something that is impossible to do with plain HTML. **Table 9.6, Table 9.7,** and **Table 9.8** show the different properties and methods you can use to change the display of an ActiveX control.

In the following steps you create a label that is a hyperlink. It appears like normal text until the user moves the mouse pointer over it. At that point, it will turn blue and underlined. Additionally, you will set some of the control's properties using VBScript when the page first loads.

(*Continued on the next page.*)

Table 9.8 Events of the Label ActiveX control.

EVENT	OCCURS WHEN
Click	the user clicks the label
Change	the label's caption changes
DblClick	the user double-clicks the label
MouseDown (Button, Shift, x, y)	the user presses the mouse button down while the pointer is over the control
MouseMove (Button, Shift, x, y)	the user moves the mouse pointer over the label
MouseUp (Button, Shift, x, y)	the user releases the mouse button while the pointer is over the control

(Continued from the previous page.)

To use the Label control:

1. Create a new, blank HTML file and save it as label.html

2. Add code within the body section, as shown in **Script 9.5**.

3. Add the script section shown in **Script 9.6** to set a few of the Label's properties.

4. Add event handlers for the **MouseDown** and **MouseUp** events, in the same script section, as shown in **Script 9.7**.

5. Save the file and load it in your browser. The result should resemble **Figure 9.9**.

Script 9.7 The **MouseDown** event occurs when the user clicks the button; **MouseUp** occurs when the button is released.

```
File  Edit  Search  Help

<SCRIPT LANGUAGE="VBSCRIPT">
<!--
  Sub Window_onLoad
    lblMicrosoft.Caption = "Microsoft"
    lblMicrosoft.FontName = "Times New Roman"
  End Sub

Sub lblMicrosoft_MouseDown(Button, Shift, x, y)
  lblMicrosoft.FontUnderline = 1
End Sub

Sub lblMicrosoft_MouseUp(Button, Shift, x, y)
  lblMicrosoft.FontUnderline = 0
  top.location.href = "http://www.microsoft.com"
End Sub
-->
</SCRIPT>
</BODY>
</HTML>
```

Script 9.5 Create a default Label control with no properties set explicitly.

```
File  Edit  Search  Help

<HTML>
<HEAD><TITLE>Using the Label
control</TITLE></HEAD>

<BODY BGCOLOR="#FFFFFF">

<OBJECT ID="lblMicrosoft" WIDTH=75 HEIGHT=20
      CLASSID="CLSID:99B42120-6EC7-11CF-A6C7-
00AA00A47DD2">
</OBJECT>

</BODY>
</HTML>
```

Script 9.6 This event handler will set the Label's **Caption** and **FontName** properties.

```
File  Edit  Search  Help

<HTML>
<HEAD><TITLE>Using the Label
control</TITLE></HEAD>

<BODY BGCOLOR="#FFFFFF">

<OBJECT ID="lblMicrosoft" WIDTH=75 HEIGHT=20
      CLASSID="CLSID:99B42120-6EC7-11CF-A6C7-
00AA00A47DD2">
</OBJECT>

<SCRIPT LANGUAGE="VBSCRIPT">
<!--
  Sub Window_onLoad
    lblMicrosoft.Caption = "Microsoft"
    lblMicrosoft.FontName = "Times New Roman"
  End Sub
-->
</SCRIPT>
</BODY>
</HTML>
```

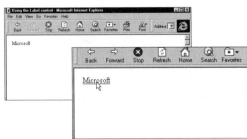

Figure 9.9 When you hold the mouse button down, the label caption appears to underline, like a hyperlink. Release the button and the Microsoft Web site loads.

USING THE LABEL CONTROL

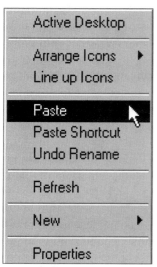

Figure 9.10
A typical Windows 95 pop-up menu.

USING THE POPUP MENU CONTROL

The **Popup** menu control displays a pop-up menu similar to the ones you see in Windows 95. The pop-up menu appears whenever the control's **Popup** method is called. The trick here is that the pop-up menu isn't normally seen on the page: you make it appear by clicking on another element, such as a form button or a graphic image. All you have to do is handle that element's **onClick** event and call the pop-up menu's **Popup** method and your menu will display.

So what might you use a pop-up menu for? If you've ever visited Microsoft's SiteBuilder pages, you'll notice they use pop-up menus linked to small arrow graphics to provide a list of choices. When you select a choice, a new page loads, as shown in **Figure 9.11.**

In the following steps, you create a **Popup** menu control that emulates this behavior.

(Continued on the next page.)

Table 9.9 Properties of the Popup menu ActiveX control.

PROPERTY	WHAT IT DOES
ItemCount	the read-only value identifying the number of menu items in the menu

Table 9.10 Methods of the Popup menu ActiveX control.

METHOD	WHAT IT DOES
AboutBox	displays an About box for the control
AddItem(addstring, index)	adds the menu item identified by the addstring parameter at the index position identified by the index parameter. If index is left out, the item is added at the end of the menu
Clear	erases all menu items
PopUp(x, y)	pops up the menu at the window coordinates identified by x and y. If no x,y coordinate values are passed, the menu appears at the current mouse pointer position
RemoveItem(index)	removes the menu item found at the index location

Table 9.11 Events of the Popup menu ActiveX control.

EVENT	OCCURS WHEN
Click(item)	The menu item specified by the item parameter is chosen by the user.

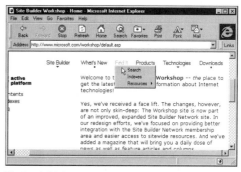

Figure 9.11 A Popup menu ActiveX control in action on the Microsoft Web site.

(Continued from the previous page.)

To use the Popup menu control:

1. Create a new, blank HTML file and save it as **popupmenu.html**

2. Add the code shown in **Script 9.8** to the body section.

3. At this point, the pop-up menu will display when you click the image, but you'll need to handle the event that occurs when the pop-up menu is clicked. This is done with the **Click** event handler shown in **Script 9.9**. Add this script section above the body section.

4. Now save your file and load it in your browser. The result should resemble **Figure 9.12**.

Tip:

■ The element you click to display the pop-up menu is up to you; it can be a button, an image, or even another ActiveX control like a **Label**.

Script 9.9 The **Select Case** block will handle each of the menu items being clicked by loading a specific Web page.

```
File   Edit   Search   Help
<HTML>
<HEAD><TITLE>Using the Popup
Menu control</TITLE></HEAD>

<SCRIPT LANGUAGE="VBSCRIPT">
<!--
  Sub Popup1_Click(x)
    Select Case x
      Case 1: top.location.href =
"http://www.bigtent.com"
        Case 2: top.location.href =
"http://www.hipmama.com"
        Case 3: top.location.href =
"http://www.internet-nexus.com"
        Case 4: top.location.href =
"http://www.lofy.com"
      End Select
  End Sub
-->
</SCRIPT>

<BODY BGCOLOR="#FFFFFF">
```

Script 9.8 This code creates the Popup menu control and displays a small arrow GIF image on the Web page. The **PARAM** tags in the **<OBJECT>** set determines each menu item in the menu.

```
File   Edit   Search   Help
<HTML>
<HEAD><TITLE>Using the Popup
Menu control</TITLE></HEAD>

<BODY BGCOLOR="#FFFFFF">

<OBJECT ID="Popup1" TYPE="application/
x-oleobject"
      CODEBASE="http://activex.microsoft.com/
controls/iexplorer/iemenu.ocx#Version=4,70,0,1161"
    CLASSID="clsid:7823A620-9DD9-11CF-A662-
00AA00C066D2"
      WIDTH=0 HEIGHT=0>
    <PARAM NAME="Menuitem[0]" VALUE="Big Tent
Media Labs">
    <PARAM NAME="Menuitem[1]" VALUE="Hip Mama">
    <PARAM NAME="Menuitem[2]" VALUE="Internet
Nexus">
    <PARAM NAME="Menuitem[3]" VALUE="Looking Out
For Yourself">
</OBJECT>

<IMG SRC="click.gif" WIDTH=8 HEIGHT=8
OnClick="Call Popup1.Popup">

</BODY>
</HTML>
```

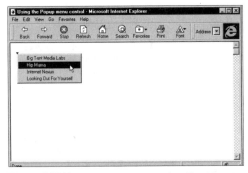

Figure 9.12 Your own pop-up menu, just like the one Microsoft uses. Clicking each menu item will load a different Web page: this should be easy to adapt to your own needs.

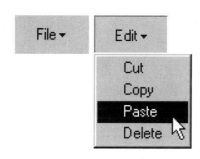

Figure 9.13 Two menu controls on the Microsoft Web site.

Table 9.12 Properties of the Menu ActiveX control.

PROPERTY	WHAT IT DOES
ItemCount	contains the number of menu items in the menu (read only)
Caption	determines the caption of the menu

Table 9.13 Properties of the Menu ActiveX control.

METHOD	WHAT IT DOES
AboutBox	displays an About box for the control
Popup(x, y)	displays the menu at the window coordinates specified by x and y. If x and y are left out, the menu is displayed at the current position of the mouse pointer
Clear	erases all menu items
RemoveItem(index)	removes the item at the position identified by index
AddItem(addstring, index)	adds a new menu item identified by addstring at the position identified by index. If index is left out, the new item is added at the end of the menu.

Table 9.14 Events of the Menu ActiveX control.

EVENT	OCCURS WHEN
Select(item)	menu item identified by item is selected
Click	menu button is clicked and no menu items are present

USING THE MENU CONTROL

The Menu control, sometimes referred to as the "button menu," provides a menu button that can be clicked to display a menu. This is somewhat similar to the menus used in Windows applications, with a slight difference: the menu control buttons display small down-arrows next to their captions to indicate visually that they provide pull-down menus, as shown in **Figure 9.13.**

You might use the Menu control instead of a Popup menu control if you know you want the menu connected to buttons. It's also a little easier to program than the Popup menu control, because you don't have to "connect" it to another element on the page.

In the following steps, you create a Menu control that changes the background color of the document. You can just as easily have each item in the menu load a new Web page, as you did in the previous Popup menu example.

(Continued on the next page.)

USING THE MENU CONTROL

(*Continued from the previous page.*)

To use the Menu control:

1. Create a new, blank HTML file and save it as **menu.html**

2. Add the **<OBJECT>** code to the body section, as shown in **Script 9.10.**

3. Now, you'll need to handle the event that occurs when a menu item is selected. This is done with the **Select** event. Add the script section shown in **Script 9.11** above the body section.

4. Save the file and load it in your browser. Your Menu control allows you to set the color of the background, as shown in **Figure 9.14.**

Note:

- Don't forget that you can copy all of the code for these examples from:

  http://www.internet-nexus.com/vbvqs

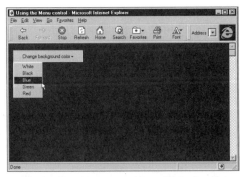

Figure 9.14 The Menu control has a 3D look and also responds to the mouse passing over it.

Script 9.10 This code creates your Menu control.

```
File  Edit  Search  Help

<HTML>
<HEAD><TITLE>Using the Menu control</TITLE></HEAD>

<BODY BGCOLOR="#FFFFFF">

<OBJECT ID="Menu1"
        CLASSID="CLSID:52DFAE60-CEBF-11CF-A3A9-
00A0C9034920"
        CODEBASE="http://activex.microsoft.com/
controls/iexplorer/btnmenu.ocx#Version=4,70,0,1161"
        TYPE="application/x-oleobject" WIDTH=180
HEIGHT=30>
   <PARAM NAME="Caption" VALUE="Change background
color">
   <PARAM NAME="Menuitem[0]" VALUE="White">
   <PARAM NAME="Menuitem[1]" VALUE="Black">
   <PARAM NAME="Menuitem[2]" VALUE="Blue">
   <PARAM NAME="Menuitem[3]" VALUE="Green">
   <PARAM NAME="Menuitem[4]" VALUE="Red">
</OBJECT>

</BODY>
</HTML>
```

Script 9.11 This Select Case block handles each of the menu items being selected by changing the color of the background to the proper value.

```
File  Edit  Search  Help

<HTML>
<HEAD><TITLE>Using the Menu control</TITLE></HEAD>

<SCRIPT LANGUAGE="VBSCRIPT">
<!--
   Sub Menu1_Select(x)
      Select Case x
         Case 1: Document.bgColor = "White"
         Case 2: Document.bgColor = "Black"
         Case 3: Document.bgColor = "Blue"
         Case 4: Document.bgColor = "Green"
         Case 5: Document.bgColor = "Red"
      End Select
   End Sub
-->
</SCRIPT>

<BODY BGCOLOR="#FFFFFF">

<OBJECT ID="Menu1"
        CLASSID="CLSID:52DFAE60-CEBF-11CF-A3A9-
00A0C9034920"
        CODEBASE="http://activex.microsoft.com/
controls/iexplorer/btnmenu.ocx#Version=4,70,0,1161"
```

ACTIVEX
CONTROL PAD

10

ActiveX Control Pad is an application program that makes it easier to add Active content such as VBScript and ActiveX controls to your Web pages. Previously, Web designers could only "hard code" these features. Now, Control Pad gives you a visual environment that uses plain English and easy-to-understand lists.

Control Pad includes a simple text editor, an ActiveX object editor, and a Script Wizard for handling ActiveX control events with VBScript code. ActiveX Control Pad makes it easy to access the ActiveX controls that are registered on your system and insert these controls into your own Web pages.

This chapter shows how to use Control Pad and explores a few of the many controls that Microsoft includes with Internet Explorer.

INSTALLING ACTIVEX CONTROL PAD

First, you need to get a copy of ActiveX Control Pad and load it onto your computer. Fortunately, it's free and available from Microsoft's Web site.

To install ActiveX Control Pad:

1. Navigate to http://www.microsoft.com/ workshop/author/cpad/download.htm with your Web browser, as shown in **Figure 10.1.**

2. Download **setuppad.exe** and **setupipn.exe** to your desktop.

3. When the downloads are complete, double-click **setuppad.exe** to install the main components.

4. Install the application to the location you desire.

5. Double-click **setupipn.exe** to install the additional components. When installation is complete, you may run ActiveX Control Pad by selecting it from the Start menu, as shown in **Figure 10.2.**

Tips:

- As always, links on the Web are subject to change. If the links mentioned above are invalid, you can download the ActiveX Control Pad from

  http://www.internet-nexus.com/vbvqs

- You can delete the **setuppad.exe** and **setupipn.exe** files from your desktop after you have installed them.

- You can also uninstall ActiveX Control Pad later if you decide to. Open the Control Panel, double-click on Add/Remove Programs, and choose Microsoft ActiveX Control Panel from the list.

Table 10.1 Here are some online resources with information about ActiveX Control Pad.

LOCATION	WHAT'S THERE
http://www.microsoft.com/ workshop/author/cpad/cpad.htm	The ActiveX Control Pad Web site
http://www.microsoft.com/ workshop/author/cpad/ download.htm	The ActiveX Control Pad download page, with various tutorials, FAQs, and white papers
http://internet-nexus.com/vbvqs	Check our site for regular updates to information as well as updated links to other sites

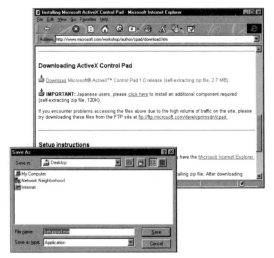

Figure 10.1 Download the installation files to your desktop.

Figure 10.2 When the installation is complete, you can launch ActiveX Control Pad from the Start menu.

INSTALLING THE ACTIVEX CONTROL PAD

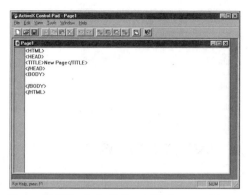

Figure 10.3 The ActiveX Control Pad opens with a blank HTML document.

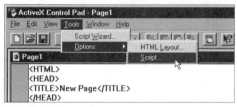

Figure 10.4 The Script sub-menu in the Tools menu allows you to choose options for the ActiveX Control Pad Script Wizard.

Figure 10.5 The ActiveX Control Pad also supports JavaScript and provides a no-code view for non-programmers.

SETTING UP ACTIVEX CONTROL PAD

ActiveX Control Pad has four major components: the text editor you see when the program first loads, the Object editor, the Script Wizard, and the HTML Layout control. Generally, you should continue editing most HTML in your text editor or HTML editor of choice, and use the ActiveX Control Pad for inserting ActiveX controls and scripting only. The Control Pad text editor lacks even the most basic editor functionality, such as font selection and auto-indent.

Before you start adding ActiveX controls to your Web pages, you should make sure that VBScript is set up as the default scripting language.

To set VBScript as the default scripting language:

1. Start ActiveX Control Pad.

2. Select the Script sub-menu item from the Options item in the Tools menu. The Script Options dialog box appears, as shown in **Figure 10.5.**

3. Choose Code View in the top pane and Visual Basic Scripting Edition in the bottom pane.

4. Close the dialog box.

Tip:

■ Choosing List view or Code view in this dialog box determines the default setting for the ActiveX Control Pad. You can switch back and forth between List view and Code view while using the Script Wizard any time you'd like.

INSERTING AN ACTIVEX CONTROL

When you first open ActiveX Control Pad, a sample HTML page is created to allow you to get to work immediately. Typically, when you are creating Web pages, you will want to load in a page you have already created and insert the appropriate ActiveX controls and scripting. For now, however, this blank HTML page is perfect for learning how to use the Control Pad.

To insert your first ActiveX Control with Control Pad:

1. Position the cursor between the <BODY> and </BODY> tags.

2. Choose Insert ActiveX Control from the Edit menu. The Insert ActiveX Control dialog box appears, as shown in **Figure 10.7.**

3. Choose Microsoft IE 30 Label Control from the list. The Object editor appears. This editor contains two windows: an Edit ActiveX Control window and a Properties window. The edit window is a visual form that displays the ActiveX control. As you change its properties from the Properties window, the Edit window will reflect those changes, as shown in **Figure 10.8.**

4. Position the windows if necessary and resize the label control by dragging it with the mouse cursor.

5. Click the Caption property in the Properties window. The label caption **Default** appears in the edit box at the top of the window, as shown in **Figure 10.9.**

Figure 10.6 Control Pad allows you to add ActiveX controls by using simple pull down menus.

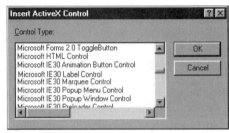

Figure 10.7 The Insert ActiveX Control dialog box lists every ActiveX control that you have on your computer.

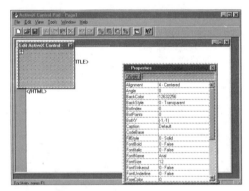

Figure 10.8 The Object editor.

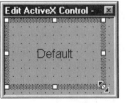

Figure 10.9 As you can see, the default caption for the label control is *Default.*

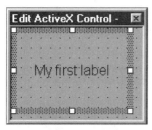

Figure 10.10 Your first label.

Figure 10.11 The HTML source code for the label control is automatically inserted into your new Web page.

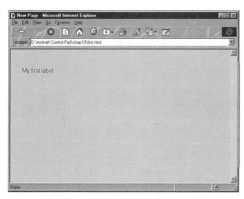

Figure 10.12 Your final result should look like this in your browser.

Figure 10.13 The icons in the left-hand margin allow you to switch between windows.

6. Highlight the text in the edit box and type **My first label**. When you hit return, the edit window changes to display the new caption as shown in **Figure 10.10**.

7. Close the Object editor by clicking the Close window button on the edit window. You are returned to the Control Pad text editor.

8. Save the file as **first.html** and then load it in your browser. The result should resemble **Figure 10.12**.

Tips:

■ If you close the Properties window by mistake, you can re-display it by double clicking the edit window.

■ You can also insert a control by right-clicking the editor window and choosing Insert ActiveX Control from the pop-up menu.

■ Once you have inserted an ActiveX control into your HTML file, you can reload the visual editor. Click the small Edit ActiveX Control icon, in the ActiveX Control Pad text editor's gutter to the left of the source code, for the ActiveX control, as shown in **Figure 10.13**.

■ To delete an ActiveX control, just select the entire control code block in the HTML source code file and press Delete. Make sure you get everything between and including the **<OBJECT>** and **</OBJECT>** tags.

USING SCRIPT WIZARD

Once you have inserted an ActiveX control, you will want to handle its events using scripts. This is done using the Script Wizard.

The Script Wizard window contains three panes: an Event pane, an Action pane, and a View pane. The upper two panes, Events and Actions, list the objects on your page and their corresponding events, methods, and properties. The view pane is where you add code.

To open the Script Wizard:

1. Open the file first.html that you created in the previous section.

2. From the Tools menu, select Script Wizard. The Script Wizard appears, as shown in **Figure 10.14.**

The Events and Action panes behave like regular Windows 95 folders. You can expand and collapse the list of available options by clicking the box next to the object.

3. Expand the events for **IeLabel1**, as shown in **Figure 10.15.** Notice the different types of events you can control, such as when the label is clicked or passed over with the mouse.

4. Expand the actions for **IeLabel1**. Notice the variety of attributes that you can control, as shown in **Figure 10.16.**

Tips:

■ Each page automatically contains the **Window** object and its **onLoad** and **onUnLoad** events.

■ In addition to the **Window** and label control objects, the Action pane contains a Go To Page action, and options to declare new global variables and procedures.

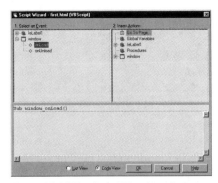

Figure 10.14 The Script Wizard window contains three panes: an **Event** pane, an **Action** pane, and a **View** pane. The view pane will display in List view or Code view, depending on your preference.

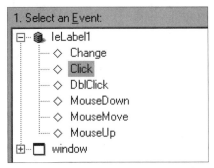

Figure 10.15 The Event pane displays all of the events that the objects in your Web page support.

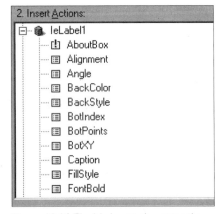

Figure 10.16 The label control contains the list of properties you saw earlier in the Object editor.

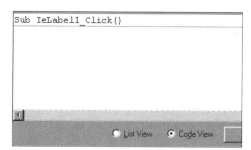

Figure 10.17 Below the View pane are two radio buttons that allow you to switch between List and Code views.

Figure 10.18 The small VBScript procedure has been added to your HTML code.

The View pane **(Figure 10.17)** changes its display based on the options selected in the upper panes. If you click the Change event in the Events page, for example, the View pane will create a procedure to handle that event. The View pane is where you add your code.

To create a script in the View pane:

1. Open first.html

2. Click the plus sign next to the **IeLabel1** object in the Event pane to expose all of the events available to the control.

3. Choose **Click**

4. Double-click the Go To Page action in the Action pane. The **OnClick** event handler now displays

   Sub IeLabel1_Click() Window.location.href = ""

5. Change the second line to read

   Window.location.href = "http://www.microsoft.com"

   to turn the label into a hyperlink.

6. Click OK. The Script Wizard closes and you are returned to the text editor where the script appears, as shown in **Figure 10.18**.

7. Save the file and load it in your browser. When you click the label, the Microsoft home page loads.

Tips:

■ Once you add scripting to your HTML file, you can reload Script Wizard by clicking the small Edit Scripts icon in the ActiveX Control Pad text editor's gutter to the left of the source code for the ActiveX control.

■ Procedures generated by Script Wizard will automatically add **End Sub** at the end of the block. You do not need to add this command yourself.

USING SCRIPT WIZARD FOR WINDOW EVENTS

Although you should use the Properties window in the Object editor to set as many control properties as possible, you will often need to change the values of these properties at run-time. One good time to do this is when the page first loads. In this example, you change the caption and some of the font properties of the label control when the Web page loads.

Figure 10.19 The **onLoad** procedure for the window object appears in the View pane.

To handle the window object's onLoad event:

1. Click the Edit Scripts icon in the gutter of the Control Pad text editor to open the Script Wizard.

2. Expand the window object in the Events pane and choose **onLoad**.

3. Expand the **IeLabel1** object in the Actions pane and double-click the **FontItalic** property. The code **IeLabel1.FontItalic** appears in the View pane. as shown in **Figure 10.20.**

4. Change the code in the event handler to

   IeLabel1.FontItalic = True

5. Press return and then double-click the FontUnderline property and change the code in the event handler to

   IeLabel1.FontUnderline = True

6. Click OK, save the document, and load it in your browser. The result should resemble **Figure 10.21**.

Tip:

■ You can switch Script Wizard into List view to edit event handlers visually, rather than using scripting. This method is OK for simple operations, but you will need to understand VBScript to create more complex effects.

Figure 10.20 Change the **FontItalic** property to read **True**.

Figure 10.21 The label's format changes at runtime.

Figure 10.22 Script Wizard supports List view, which provides English-like explanations of event handlers and the actions they take.

Figure 10.23 Insert a **<P>** after the **</OBJECT>** tag.

Figure 10.24 Change the Caption property to **Click me!**

Figure 10.25 The label control has a height of **30**, a width of **200**, no caption, and its alignment is centered to the left.

USING MULTIPLE CONTROLS

You will often need to have more than one control on a Web page. If the layout is simple, you can just insert the controls with the Control Pad as you have done previously. Typical forms pages, for example, are created this way. Of course, you can only insert one control at a time, but there is no logical limit to the number of ActiveX controls you can include on a Web page. In the following example, you will construct a simple page with three ActiveX controls: a text box that accepts user input, a command button, and a label that outputs the text from the text box when the command button is clicked.

To add multiple controls:

1. Create a blank Web page and insert a Microsoft Forms 2.0 TextBox control. Set its Width property to **200**

2. Close the Object editor to return to the text editor. Insert a **<P>** tag after the **</OBJECT>** tag, as shown in **Figure 10.23,** and press return.

3. Insert a Microsoft Forms 2.0 Command-Button control. Change the Caption property to read **Click me!** as shown in **Figure 10.24.**

4. Close the Object editor and insert another **<P>** tag, this time following the **</OBJECT>** tag associated with the command button control you inserted. Press return.

5. Insert a Microsoft IE30 Label control. Set the following property values.

Height	30
Width	200
Caption	(blank)
Alignment	3-Left Centered

(*Continued on the next page.*)

USING MULTIPLE CONTROLS

(Continued from the previous page.)

6. Once again, close the Object editor. Now, you can add some scripting to tie the controls together.

7. Open the Script Wizard by choosing Script Wizard from the Tools menu.

8. Expand the entry for **CommandButton1** in the Event pane and select **Click**. A procedure for the **Click** event will appear in the View pane.

9. Type the following code into the View pane:

leLabel1.Caption = TextBox1.Text.

When the button is clicked, this code will load the text from the text box into the caption of the label control. The **Text** property of the text box contains the text typed there by the user.

10. Press OK in Script Wizard and save the document. Test it with your browser. The result should resemble **Figure 10.26.**

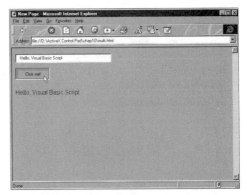

Figure 10.26 When the button is clicked, text from the text box loads into the caption of the label control.

Tips:

- When you add controls to your Web pages with Control Pad, you must still deal with the limitations of HTML. For more complex designs with multiple controls, use the HTML Layout control, a container for other ActiveX controls. The HTML Layout control is discussed later in this chapter.

- There seems to be a bug in the current version of Control Pad. If you create multiple instances of the same type of control (two command buttons, for example), it will create the two controls with the same ID property. If you are placing more than one instance of any control on your Web pages, make sure you give each one a unique identifier.

USING MULTIPLE CONTROLS

XRT

Item1	Value1	Value2	...
Item2	Value1	Value2	...
Item3	Value1	Value2	...

Figure 10.27 The text of the data file for the stock ticker control is fairly simple. Remember to hit return at the end of each line. Only the Item entries are required for each line: each value is optional and you can have as many values for each item as you wish.

USING THE STOCK TICKER CONTROL

The stock ticker control will be especially appealing to financial sites, but it can also be used as a general-purpose text marquee, similar to the <MARQUEE> HTML tag. The stock ticker continuously displays scrolling data. This data resides in a text file or a special XRT file at a URL you identify and can change constantly—the stock ticker updates the display automatically to reflect the changing data. You can also determine how often the stock ticker updates itself.

For purposes of this example, we will be using a simple text file (with a .TXT or .DAT extension) to hold the data for the stock ticker. The XRT file format mentioned above is fairly complex and specialized. The text data file should look something like **Figure 10.27.**

As the data in the text file is scrolled through the stock ticker, it rolls over and redisplays at the beginning once the end of the data is reached. Conceivably, this data file could be quite large, but small files work equally well.

(Continued on the next page.)

USING THE STOCK TICKER CONTROL

(*Continued from the previous page.*)

To create the data file:

1. Open the folder that will contain the data file.

2. Right-click the background and choose New and then text file from the shortcut menu.

3. Name the file **data.txt**

4. Open the text file and type the following, making sure to separate the entries on each line with a tab:

   XRT

My Stock	+1	112.5
Microsoft	+10.25	125.6
Apple	+.1	33.5
Otherstock	-0.2	11.3

5. Save the file and exit Notepad.

6. Upload the file to your Web site as you would with any other file.

To use the stock ticker control:

1. Insert the Microsoft IE30 Stock Ticker Control onto a Web page with Control Pad. The Object editor appears.

2. Set the following property values:

Height	50
Width	600
DataObjectActive	1
DataObjectVisible	1
DataObjectName	URL (such as http://mydomain.com/data.txt)
ScrollWidth	5

   You can see the stock ticker start working right in the Object editor, as shown in **Figure 10.28.**

3. Close the Object editor, save the file and view it with your browser. The result should resemble **Figure 10.29.**

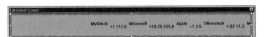

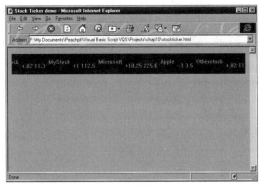

Figure 10.28 The Stock Ticker control is working in design time, allowing you to see how it will behave when the user sees it.

Figure 10.29 Your stock ticker masterpiece in action.

Figure 10.30 Though the Timer control appears in the Object editor, it will not be visible to the user when the page is loaded.

USING THE TIMER CONTROL

The timer control is invisible at run-time (that is, when someone is viewing your Web page), but it allows you to execute lines of script at specific timed intervals. The most important property, Interval, specifies the amount of time that goes by between each timer event. It is specified in milliseconds, so a value of 500 is about half a second. Don't use the timer for anything critical, however: its timeliness is not guaranteed. The Timer event occurs every time the value of Interval is reached: if Interval is 500, a Timer event is triggered twice every second. You can place code in the timer control's Timer event handler and this code will execute every time the timer event is triggered.

In this example, you create a cool spinning text label, using the label control's Angle property to redisplay the label periodically, creating an animation effect.

To use the timer control:

1. Create a new web page and insert a label control. Set the following property values:

Height	200
Width	200
Caption	Watch me spin!
ForeColor	&H00FF00FF

2. Close the Object editor and insert a Microsoft IE30 Timer Control below the label (it doesn't really matter where you put it, since the timer will be invisible when the page loads). The Object editor opens.

3. Change the timer's **Interval** property to 200 and close the Object editor. Now you must bind the label to the timer so that the label changes every time the **Timer** event triggers.

4. Open Script Wizard and select the **Timer** event for **IeTimer1** in the Event pane. The event handler procedure for the **Timer** event appears in the View pane as shown in **Figure 10.31**.

5. In the Actions pane, expand **IeLabel1** and double-click the **Angle** property. The code **IeLabel1.Angle** appears in the View pane. Change the code to read

   ```
   if IeLabel1.Angle < 370 then

       IeLabel1.Angle = IeLabel1.Angle + 10

       else IeLabel1.Angle = 0

   end if
   ```

   This will spin the label control 10 degrees every time the **Timer** event is triggered. Since the label is redrawn every time you change the **Angle** property, it appears to spin in place!

6. Click OK to close the Script Wizard.

7. Save the file and load it in your browser. The result should resemble **Figure 10.32**.

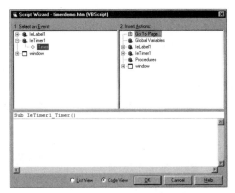

Figure 10.31 The handler for the Timer event determines what occurs at each Interval.

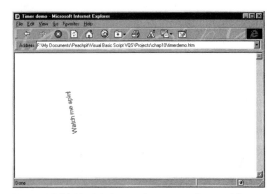

Figure 10.32 The label control continuously spins 10 degrees at a time.

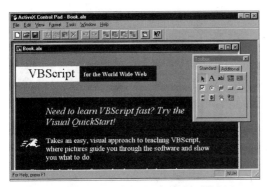

Figure 10.33 People with paper-based publishing backgrounds should feel right at home with this tool.

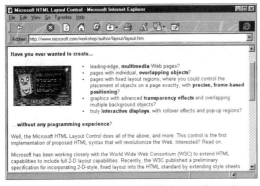

Figure 10.34 Microsoft has an HTML Layout Control home page at http://www.microsoft.com/workshop/author/layout/layout.htm

USING THE HTML LAYOUT CONTROL

If you need finer control over the layout of the controls on your Web page, you can use the HTML Layout control, an ActiveX control that implements 2-D frame-based layouts and is compatible with new HTML standards. The ActiveX Control Pad installs the HTML Layout control and includes a special editor that allows you to create HTML layouts.

The HTML Layout control is a blank frame that is used to contain other ActiveX controls. It provides precise placement of those controls in the X, Y, and Z coordinate systems. That is, it supports a z-order, where controls overlap and contain transparency information. This placement of controls can change at run-time, so that they can appear to move or animate if desired. This effect also allows the user to interact with controls on a page and move them with the mouse. As with other ActiveX controls, you can control the HTML Layout control's properties and methods with VBScript.

ActiveX Control Pad includes an HTML Layout editor that allows you to visually place controls in a layout, similar to Visual Basic and desktop publishing programs. In fact, the toolbox palette used in the Layout editor is very similar to the palette controls used in desktop publishing. Once you have created the desired layout, you save the layout to disk and insert it into a Web page just like any other control. Layout control files end in an .ALX extension.

Every control you place in the HTML Layout control can be accessed from Script Wizard, in the same manner that you've used to access other controls. The graphic effects that are possible with the HTML Layout control rival those in paper-based desktop publishing systems, with multiple levels of overlapping and transparency effects.

To create an HTML layout:

1. Choose New HTML Layout from the File menu. The layout editor appears and a new menu item, Format, is added to the Control Pad menu bar, as shown in **Figure 10.35.**

2. Place a command button on the layout, as shown in **Figure 10.36.**

3. Right-click the command button and choose Properties. The familiar Properties window appears.

4. Change the caption of the command button to read

   Click me!

5. Place an Image control on the layout and stretch it out to fill the whole layout. Open the Properties window if it is closed and make the following property changes:

   PictureSizeMode = Clip

   PictureTiling = True

   PicturePath = A path of a valid image that will look good tiled.

6. Once this is done, the image should be tiled across the entire layout, as shown in **Figure 10.37.** Of course, now the command button is hidden, so you will have to move the image control visually to the back.

Figure 10.35 The Format menu contains layout options.

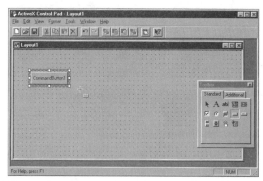

Figure 10.36 If you aren't sure which tool is which in the Toolbox, let your mouse pointer hover over each tool and a ToolTip will appear, identifying the tool.

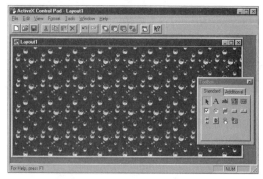

Figure 10.37 The image tiles the entire background.

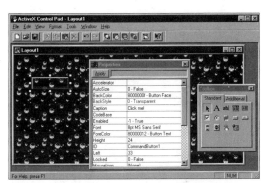

Figure 10.38 You can now see the background image through the button.

Figure 10.39

7. Right-click the image control and choose Move Backward. The command button reappears.

8. Select the command button and change **BackStyle** property to **0-Transparent (Figure 10.38)**.

9. Place another image control on the layout. Again, set the **PicturePath** property to a valid image file, set the PictureTiling to **True**, and change its **Height** and **Width** properties to match the height and width of the command button.

10. Move the new image file so that it covers the command button and right-click it.

11. Choose Move Backward, as shown in **Figure 10.39.**

12. You may need to change the Font color of the command button's caption to a lighter color. To do this, change the command button's **ForeColor** property in the Properties window.

13. Save your HTML Layout by choosing Save from the File menu. Close the HTML Layout editor.

Tips:

- If you place a control on the layout you wish to delete, just right-click that control on the layout and choose Delete.

- If you use image controls in an HTML layout and plan to use that layout on the Web, remember to upload the graphics as well.

INSERTING AN HTML LAYOUT INTO A WEB PAGE

Creating an HTML Layout is all well and good, but you must insert it into a Web page before you can view it in a Web document. Inserting an HTML Layout is straightforward and very similar to inserting a single ActiveX control.

To insert an HTML Layout:

1. Create a new, blank Web page by selecting New HTML from the File menu.

2. Choose Insert HTML Layout from the Edit menu, as shown in **Figure 10.40.**

3. Open the layout you just created. The code is placed in your HTML file, as shown in **Figure 10.41.**

4. Save the HTML file and view it with your browser. The result should resemble **Figure 10.42.**

Tip:

■ The HTML Layout control makes it easy to create layouts with fixed dimensions. You should make an effort to create a layout that will display properly on most people's browsers. Many Web pages are designed at a fixed width of 600 pixels, for example.

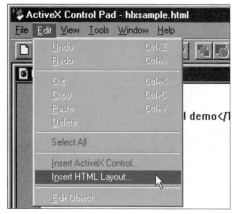

Figure 10.40 Choose Insert HTML Layout from the Edit menu.

Figure 10.41 The HTML code needed to display your layout is automatically inserted into the Web source.

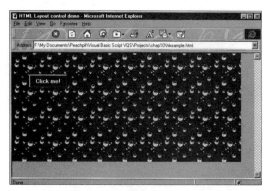

Figure 10.42 The final result.

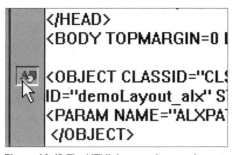

```
</HEAD>
<BODY TOPMARGIN=0

<OBJECT CLASSID="CL$
ID="demoLayout_alx" S
<PARAM NAME="ALXPA
</OBJECT>
```

Figure 10.43 The HTML Layout editor can be summoned by clicking the Edit HTML Layout icon in the gutter of the ActiveX Control Pad text editor.

USING SCRIPT WIZARD WITH HTML LAYOUT CONTROL

Every control you add to an HTML Layout can be scripted with Script Wizard. Creating a pleasant design is nice, but the goal here is an active page, and that requires some VBScript to liven things up. In this section, you will add code to your command button so that it responds to mouse clicks.

To invoke Script Wizard from the HTML Layout editor:

1. Return to the ActiveX Control Pad and click the Edit HTML Layout icon in the gutter of the text editor **(Figure 10.43)**. The HTML Layout editor appears.

2. Right-click the command button and choose Script Wizard.

3. In the Event pane, expand Command Button1 and Choose Click.

4. Double-click Go To Page in the Action pane and change the line of code that appears in the View pane to read

   Window.location.href = "http://www.peachpit.com"

5. Click OK to save the code and close Script Wizard.

6. Close the HTML Layout editor and save the file that contains the layout.

7. Load the file into your browser and test the command button.

Tips:

■ Use Script Wizard with the controls contained by an HTML Layout control in the same way that you use it with individual controls.

■ If you invoke Script Wizard from the Control Pad, you will not be able to access the controls contained by the layout. To access these controls, invoke Script Wizard from the HTML Layout editor.

APPENDIX A

WEB RESOURCES FOR ACTIVEX CONTROL PAD AND HTML LAYOUT CONTROL

Microsoft and other third-party sites maintain a wellspring of information about the ActiveX Control Pad and HTML Layout control. For more up-to-date sites, please refer to the Resources section of this book's Web site at **http://www.internet-nexus/vbvqs**

Active X Control Pad

The ActiveX Control Pad home page	http://www.microsoft.com/workshop/author/cpad/
ActiveX Control Pad white paper	http://www.microsoft.com/workshop/author/cpad/apad.htm
ActiveX Control Pad tutorial	http://www.microsoft.com/workshop/author/cpad/tutorial.htm
ActiveX Control Pad and HTML	http://www.microsoft.com/workshop/author/Layout Control Gallery layout/samples.htm
ActiveX Control Pad Technical Frequently Asked Questions	http://www.microsoft.com/workshop/author/cpad/newcpad.htm
ActiveXpress Control Pad tutorial	http://www.techweb.com/activexpress/

HTML Layout Control

HTML Layout Control home page	http://www.microsoft.com/workshop/author/layout/layout.htm
HTML Layout Control	http://www.microsoft.com/ie/ie3/layout.htm
HTML Layout Control Authoring Tips	http://www.microsoft.com/workshop/author/cpad/howto/container.htm
Using the HTML Layout Control	http://www.microsoft.com/ie/most/howto/layout.htm

INDEX

T

U

V

W

X, Y, Z

More from Peachpit Press

Getting Hits: The Definitive Guide to Promoting Your Website

Don Sellers

Building a world-class Web site doesn't mean people will come flocking—Web sites must be promoted to be successful. *Getting Hits* is the guidebook to the entirely new processes of advertising and publicizing that comprise promotion on the Web. Topics include: posting your site to a search engine; links that give the biggest hits; guerrilla marketing strategies; producing hits offline; creating your own Web campaign; and keeping visitors coming back to your site. *$19.95 (208 pages)*

Elements of Web Design

Darcy DiNucci, Maria Giudice and Lynne Stiles

This book introduces graphic designers to the opportunities and pitfalls of Web design. *Elements of Web Design* includes chapters on every step of assembling pages—from practical issues, such as pulling together a team with the appropriate skills and creating contracts to reflect the ever-changing nature of Web pages, to the technical and design issues involved in creating HTML, graphics, and interactivity. Full color throughout. *$39.95 (208 pages)*

HTML for the World Wide Web, 2nd Edition: Visual QuickStart Guide

Elizabeth Castro

This step-by-step guide on using HTML to design pages for the World Wide Web presumes no prior knowledge of HTML, or even the Internet. It uses clear, concise instructions for creating each element of a Web page. Expanded coverage in this edition includes such major new topics as style sheets and frames, progressive JPEG images and animated GIFs, font and column width controls. *$17.95 (192 pages)*

JavaScript for the World Wide Web: Visual QuickStart Guide

Ted Gesing and Jeremy Schneider

JavaScript is a programming language designed to be used in conjunction with HTML, making HTML more powerful and interactive. All predictions are that JavaScript will become as important as HTML, and it is now fully supported in Netscape Navigator and Microsoft Internet Explorer. While other JavaScript books are intended for experienced programmers, this one is for the vast majority of HTML coders who are less technically sophisticated but still would like a useful introduction and handy reference. *$17.95 (220 pages)*

Web Graphics Tools and Techniques

Peter Kentie

This book is an indispensable resource for Web site creators needing to master a variety of authoring and graphics tools. It begins with basic Web concepts, then proceeds into the specifics of formatting graphics, text, and tables with HTML. Next, it moves deeper into graphics techniques, explaining the use of such tools as Photoshop, Painter, Poser, KPT Welder, GIF Construction Set, and Director. Also covers advanced issues such as tables, clickable maps, 3-D images, and user interaction. Full color throughout. $39.95 (320 pages)

Order Form

USA 800-283-9444 • 510-548-4393 • fax 510-548-5991
Canada 800-387-8028 • 416-447-1779 • fax 800-456-0536 or 416-443-0948

QTY	TITLE	PRICE	TOTAL

SUBTOTAL	
ADD APPLICABLE SALES TAX*	
SHIPPING	
TOTAL	

Shipping is by UPS ground: $4 for first item, $1 each add'l.

*We are required to pay sales tax in all states with the exceptions of AK, DE, MT, NH, and OR.
Please include appropriate sales tax if you live in any state not mentioned above.

CUSTOMER INFORMATION

NAME

COMPANY

STREET ADDRESS

CITY   STATE   ZIP

PHONE (   )   FAX (   )
[REQUIRED FOR CREDIT CARD ORDERS]

PAYMENT METHOD

❏ CHECK ENCLOSED   ❏ VISA   ❏ MASTERCARD   ❏ AMEX

CREDIT CARD #   EXP. DATE

COMPANY PURCHASE ORDER #

TELL US WHAT YOU THINK

PLEASE TELL US WHAT YOU THOUGHT OF THIS BOOK: TITLE:_____

WHAT OTHER BOOKS WOULD YOU LIKE US TO PUBLISH?